The
Essential
Stitch
Collection

The Essential Stitch Collection

A Creative Guide to the **300 Stitches**
Every Knitter Really Needs to Know

LESLEY STANFIELD & MELODY GRIFFITHS

Reader's
Digest

The Reader's Digest Association, Inc.
Pleasantville, New York / Montreal / Sydney / Singapore / Mumbai

FOR QUARTO
Project Editor Emma Poulter
Art Editor Emma Clayton
Designer Julie Francis
Design Assistant Saffron Stocker
Photographers Simon Pask, David Crawford, and Phil Wilkins
Art Director Caroline Guest
Creative Director Moira Clinch
Publisher Paul Carslake

FOR READER'S DIGEST
U.S. Project Editor Candace Levy
Canadian Project Editor Jesse Corbeil
Cover and Project Designer Jennifer Tokarski
Senior Art Director George McKeon
Executive Editor, Trade Publishing Dolores York
Canadian Project Manager Pamela Johnson
Associate Publisher, Trade Publishing Rosanne McManus
President and Publisher, Trade Publishing Harold Clarke

Library of Congress Cataloging in Publication Data:
Stanfield, Lesley.
The essential stitch collection : a creative guide to the 300 stitches
every knitter really needs to know / Lesley Stanfield & Melody
Griffiths.
  p. cm.
Includes index.
ISBN 978-1-60652-043-7 (North American Edition)
ISBN 978-1-60652-183-0 (International Edition)
1. Knitting. I. Griffiths, Melody. II. Title.
TT820.S79546 2010
746.43'2--dc22
                        2009047907
We are committed to both the quality of our products and the
service we provide to our customers. We value your comments,
so please feel free to contact us.

          The Reader's Digest Association, Inc.
          Adult Trade Publishing
          Reader's Digest Road
          Pleasantville, NY 10570-7000

NOTE TO OUR READERS
The editors who produced this book have attempted to make
the contents as accurate and correct as possible. Illustrations,
photographs, and text have been carefully checked. All instructions
should be reviewed and understood by the reader before
undertaking any project.

For more Reader's Digest products and information,
visit our website:
          www.rd.com (in the United States)
          www.readersdigest.ca (in Canada)
          www.readersdigest.com.au (in Australia)
          www.readersdigest.co.nz (in New Zealand)
          www.rdasia.com (in Asia)

Color separation by Modern Age Repro House Ltd., Hong Kong
Printed in China by 1010 Printing International Ltd.

1 3 5 7 9 10 8 6 4 2

Contents

Introduction

Our collection of 300 stitch patterns is designed for hand knitters of all abilities and ambitions because it covers simple stitches that are the basis of other patterns and then develops more complex and challenging ideas. It's really hard to explain the fascination of knitting, especially to a non-knitter, and it's true there can be frustrations along the way. But once you have the mechanical aspect of making stitches under control, you are the art director. You can select colors, choose yarns, combine stitches, and be both critical and creative.

If you knit as a social activity you may want to keep to the simpler stitches and you'll find a wide variety of these in this collection. The more elaborate stitch patterns frequently require more patience than skill; experiment freely, because there is nothing more satisfying than attempting something that you thought beyond your ability and then discovering that it really wasn't all that difficult.

We have searched out some old, forgotten stitches, and have had great fun inventing many new ones in the hope that we can communicate our enthusiasm for knitting.

Enjoy the alchemy of yarn and needles!

About this book

This book features 300 stitches arranged in chapters, each color-coded so you can easily find what you want. Starting with basic textures (plains and purls), the content moves through the range of samples, ending with a collection of unusual techniques. At the back is a guide that shows you how to use the stitches for design, along with a rundown of all the essential knitting techniques.

THE DIRECTORY
Stitch selectors
Each chapter is introduced with a "Stitch selector" that displays all the samples in the chapter next to each other, so you can compare stitches.

The stitch samples
The stitch samples are organized into chapters: Knit and purl, Twists, Cables, Lace, Bobbles and leaves, Stranded and intarsia, Unusual stitches, and Letters and Numbers.

KNIT KNOW-HOW
Using the stitches
Pages 184–191: Many knitters have a whole range of stitch patterns at hand but don't know how to use them. This section shows you how to use the stitches to design for yourself, with both allover pattern repeats or more simple panels or motifs, using the book's texture and color stitches.

Essential techniques
Pages 194–199: This section includes all the essential techniques, from getting started to understanding more complex areas (like increasing and decreasing) and deciding which is the best method for the type of stitch you will be using.

Reading the charts
Pages 200–203: This section explains how to use the charts, allowing you to get the most out of the book.

Abbreviations and symbols
Pages 204–205: The most frequently used abbreviations and symbols in this book are reproduced here. Any unusual abbreviations and symbols—specific to a particular stitch pattern—are presented as "Specific symbols" alongside the chart. There's also an abbreviation reminder on the fold-out flap, opposite page 207.

Stitch selector
With each chapter's stitches laid out next to each other, it's easy to select something you like.

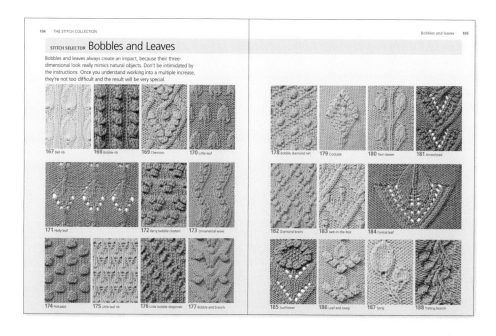

Stitch samples
Each chapter has an introductory
section containing simple designs
for beginners, including both
row-by-row written instructions
and easy-to-read charts.

Skill level
Samples are graded by skill
level on a scale of 1 to 3,
with 1 being for beginners.

Yarns used
Samples are knitted
in easy-to-view plain,
smooth yarns.

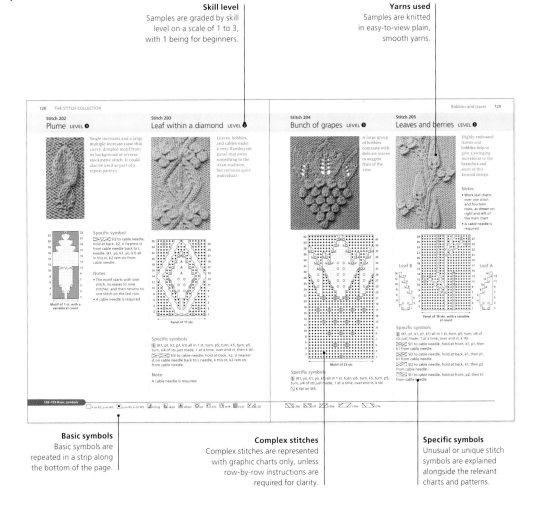

Basic symbols
Basic symbols are
repeated in a strip along
the bottom of the page.

Complex stitches
Complex stitches are represented
with graphic charts only, unless
row-by-row instructions are
required for clarity.

Specific symbols
Unusual or unique stitch
symbols are explained
alongside the relevant
charts and patterns.

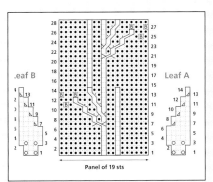

Copying the stitch charts
The stitch charts are
printed in black and white
so you can photocopy
or scan them to enlarge
them (particularly useful
if you have poor eyesight,
are working in a badly lit
space, or are knitting on
the go at a group or class).

Fold-out flap
Opposite page 207, you'll find a fold-out flap
containing the stitch abbreviations and a
needle-size conversion chart.

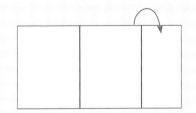

The
Stitch
Collection

This section features 300 stitches organized into chapters, each color coded and beginning with a visual stitch selector so you can easily find what you want. Starting with basic textures (plains and purls), the content moves through the range of stitch patterns before ending with a collection of unusual techniques.

STITCH SELECTOR Knit and Purl

Knit and purl stitches are the building blocks of knitting—they make stockinette and reverse stockinette stitch, many ribs, and many more textures. Understanding that the smooth V of knit is the opposite of the round blip of purl is the key to these stitches.

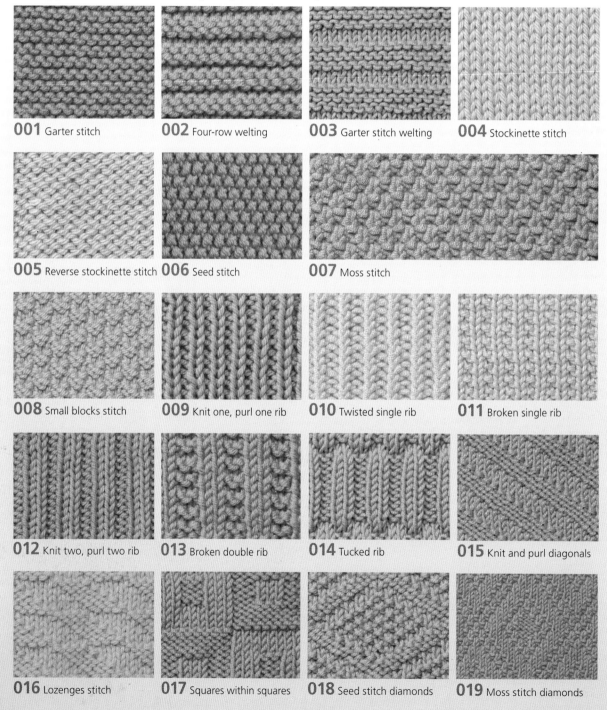

001 Garter stitch

002 Four-row welting

003 Garter stitch welting

004 Stockinette stitch

005 Reverse stockinette stitch

006 Seed stitch

007 Moss stitch

008 Small blocks stitch

009 Knit one, purl one rib

010 Twisted single rib

011 Broken single rib

012 Knit two, purl two rib

013 Broken double rib

014 Tucked rib

015 Knit and purl diagonals

016 Lozenges stitch

017 Squares within squares

018 Seed stitch diamonds

019 Moss stitch diamonds

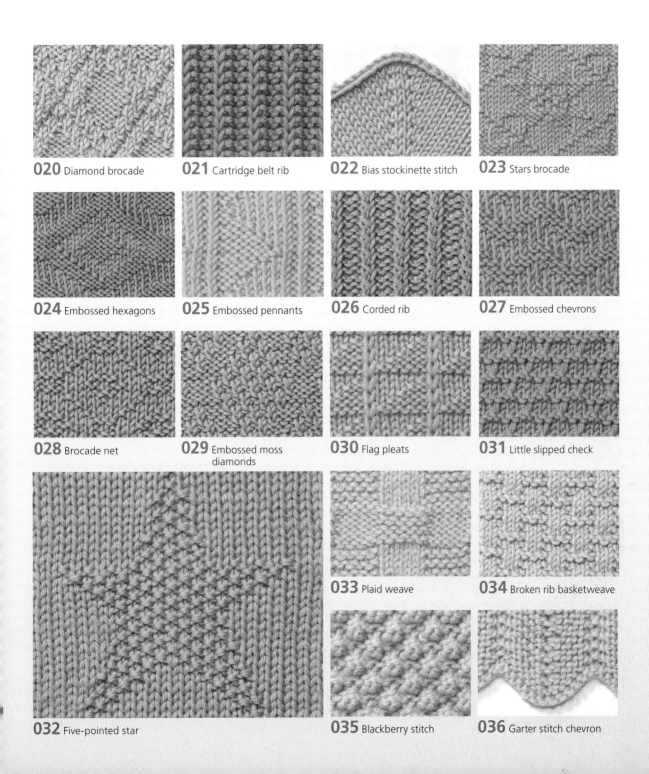

020 Diamond brocade

021 Cartridge belt rib

022 Bias stockinette stitch

023 Stars brocade

024 Embossed hexagons

025 Embossed pennants

026 Corded rib

027 Embossed chevrons

028 Brocade net

029 Embossed moss diamonds

030 Flag pleats

031 Little slipped check

032 Five-pointed star

033 Plaid weave

034 Broken rib basketweave

035 Blackberry stitch

036 Garter stitch chevron

Stitch 001
Garter stitch LEVEL ❶

Garter stitch is simple since every stitch on every row is plain knit. This produces a reversible fabric with no tendency to curl, making it useful for bands and edgings. Its knit-stitch ridges cause it to stretch slightly widthwise and contract vertically to give an almost square gauge. When counting rows, remember that there's a wrong-side row between each pair of ridges on the right side. The same garter stitch is achieved by purling every stitch on every row.

Any number of sts, shown over 5

Method

1st row (RS) K.
2nd row K.
These 2 rows form the pattern.

Stitch 002
Four-row welting LEVEL ❶

Welting is the term for a series of horizontal furrows made with a combination of rows of knit and purl. It has a tendency to stretch widthwise and can be worked over any number of stitches. This four-row version is probably the simplest.

Any number of sts, shown over 5

Method

1st row (RS) K.
2nd row P.
3rd row P.
4th row K.
These 4 rows form the pattern.

Stitch 003
Garter stitch welting LEVEL ❶

Seven of the eight pattern rows of this welting are knit. This gives it a deeper, softer texture than some other weltings.

Method

1st row (RS) K.
2nd row P.
3rd–8th rows K.
These 8 rows form the pattern.

Any number of sts, shown over 5

Stitch 004
Stockinette stitch LEVEL ❶

Stockinette stitch makes for a smooth fabric and is made by knitting all stitches on right-side rows and purling all stitches on the wrong side. It's probably the best-known and most-used stitch in knitting.

Method

1st row (RS) K.
2nd row P.
These 2 rows form the pattern.

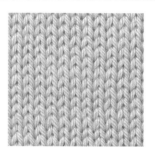

Any number of sts, shown over 5

□ k on RS, p on WS   ● p on RS, k on WS

Stitch 005
Reverse stockinette stitch LEVEL ❶

Less frequently used, but equally distinctive, reverse stockinette stitch is the opposite of stockinette stitch. Purling all stitches on right-side rows and knitting all stitches on wrong-side rows shows off the purl aspect of the stitch.

Any number of sts, shown over 5

Method

1st row (RS) P.

2nd row K.

These 2 rows form the pattern.

Stitch 006
Seed stitch LEVEL ❶

Seed stitch makes one of the simplest and most satisfying textures. Like garter stitch, it tends to stretch slightly widthwise and contract vertically to give an almost square gauge. It consists of alternate knit and purl stitches.

Multiple of 2 sts plus 1

Method

1st row (RS) [K1, p1] to last st, k1.

2nd row As 1st row.

These 2 rows form the pattern.

Note

Over an even number of stitches, work [k1, p1] to the end of the first row then [p1, k1] along the second row.

Stitch 007
Moss stitch LEVEL ❶

Sometimes called Irish moss stitch, this four-row variation on seed stitch does not have the same tendency to contract vertically. Like seed stitch it can be started with a knit or a purl stitch as long as the following knits and purls correspond.

Multiple of 2 sts plus 1

Method

1st row (RS) [K1, p1] to last st, k1.
2nd row [P1, k1] to last st, p1.
3rd row [P1, k1] to last st, p1.
4th row [K1, p1] to last st, k1.
These 4 rows form the pattern.

Stitch 008
Small blocks stitch LEVEL ❶

This is a four-row repeat like moss stitch but with the stitch multiple doubled. The result is a very different but equally simple textured stitch pattern that shows how blocks can be built up.

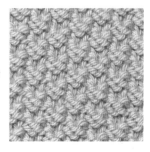

Multiple of 4 sts plus 2

Method

1st row (RS) [K2, p2] to last 2 sts, k2.
2nd row [P2, k2] to last 2 sts, p2.
3rd row [P2, k2] to last 2 sts, p2.
4th row [K2, p2] to last 2 sts, k2.
These 4 rows form the pattern.

Stitch 009
Knit one, purl one rib
LEVEL ❶

Alternating knit and purl stitches along the row gives a springy, narrow rib with a lot of uses. It can be worked over an even number of stitches, but balancing the rib by working over an odd number of stitches is more usual.

Shown over an odd number of sts; multiple of 2 sts plus 1

Method
1st row (RS) [K1, p1] to last st, k1.
2nd row [P1, k1] to last st, p1.
These 2 rows form the pattern.

Note
Over an even number of stitches, work [k1, p1] to the end of the first row then work the second row the same.

Stitch 010
Twisted single rib
LEVEL ❶

This is a variation on knit one, purl one rib, which, although it has less elasticity than the original, has a very crisp definition. The knit stitches on the right side and the purl stitches on the wrong side are worked through the back of the loop.

Multiple of 2 sts plus 1

Method
1st row (RS) [P1, k1 tbl] to last st, p1.
2nd row [K1, p1 tbl] to last st, k1.
These 2 rows form the pattern.

Stitch 011
Broken single rib
LEVEL ❶

If right-side rows are knit one, purl one but wrong-side rows are simply purl, the resulting rib has a textured appearance but very little elasticity.

Method
1st row (RS) [K1, p1] to last st, k1.
2nd row P.
These 2 rows form the pattern.

Multiple of 2 sts plus 1

Stitch 012
Knit two, purl two rib
LEVEL ❶

This classic reversible stitch is probably the most deeply furrowed of all the ribs. It's sometimes called double rib or two-and-two rib and can be used for entire garments as well as edgings.

Method
1st row (RS) [K2, p2] to last 2 sts, k2.
2nd row [P2, k2] to last 2 sts, p2.
These 2 rows form the pattern.

Multiple of 4 sts plus 2

☐ k on RS, p on WS   ● p on RS, k on WS   ◨ k tbl on RS, p tbl on WS

Stitch 013
Broken double rib
LEVEL ❶

Purling wrong-side rows introduces garter stitch verticals into knit two, purl two rib. This flattens the rib but makes a firm texture stitch.

Method
1st row (RS) [K2, p2] to last 2 sts, k2.
2nd row P.
These 2 rows form the pattern.

Multiple of 4 sts plus 2

Stitch 014
Tucked rib
LEVEL ❷

Inserting two rows of stockinette stitch between alternating bands of knit two, purl two rib produces a strongly defined texture that's quite different from plain rib.

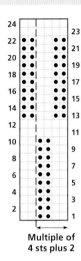
Multiple of 4 sts plus 2

Stitch 015
Knit and purl diagonals
LEVEL ❷

Groups of knit and purl stitches moved along one stitch on every row make sharply angled, very well defined diagonals.

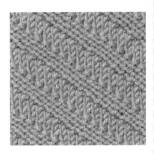

Method
1st row (RS) [K4, p4] to end.
2nd row [K3, p4, k1] to end.
3rd row [P2, k4, p2] to end.
4th row [K1, p4, k3] to end.
5th row [P4, k4] to end.
6th row [P3, k4, p1] to end.
7th row [K2, p4, k2] to end.
8th row [P1, k4, p3] to end.
These 8 rows form the pattern.

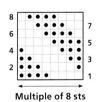
Multiple of 8 sts

Stitch 016
Lozenges stitch
LEVEL ❷

By breaking up knit and purl diagonals, a different sort of repeat pattern is made.

Method
1st row [P4, k4] to end.
2nd row [P3, k4, p1] to end.
3rd row [K2, p4, k2] to end.
4th row [P1, k4, p3] to end.
5th row [K4, p4] to end.
6th row [P4, k4] to end.
7th row [K1, p4, k3] to end.
8th row [P2, k4, p2] to end.
9th row [K3, p4, k1] to end.
10th row [K4, p4] to end.
These 10 rows form the pattern.

Multiple of 8 sts

Stitch 017
Squares within squares
LEVEL ❷

Stitch 018
Seed stitch diamonds
LEVEL ❷

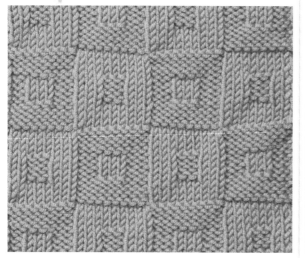

Alternating squares of knit and purl create a strong relief texture, then adding smaller squares increases the interest. Note that a square consists of more rows than stitches.

Two stitches of reverse stockinette stitch outline the seed stitch to make a very strongly embossed pattern of shallow diamonds.

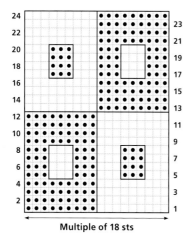

Multiple of 18 sts

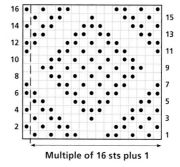

Multiple of 16 sts plus 1

☐ k on RS, p on WS ● p on RS, k on WS

Stitch 019
Moss stitch diamonds LEVEL ②

These diamonds within diamonds are constructed in moss stitch on a stockinette-stitch background. The central diamonds have a tiny panel of reverse stockinette stitch.

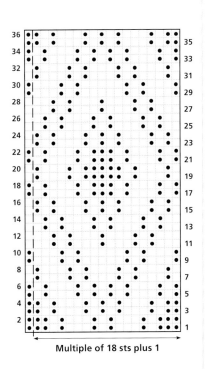

Multiple of 18 sts plus 1

Stitch 020
Diamond brocade LEVEL ②

Outlining reverse-stockinette-stitch diamonds with two stitches of stockinette stitch gives an almost quilted effect to a simple combination of knit and purl.

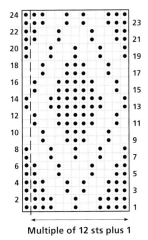

Multiple of 12 sts plus 1

Stitch 021
Cartridge belt rib LEVEL ②

This classic rib has the advantage of being reversible. The deep furrows and strong knit-stitch ridges are made by slipping stitches. Otherwise, this is a simple two-row repeat with no purl stitches.

Multiple of 4 sts plus 3

Specific symbol
⊟ Wyif sl1 purlwise.

Method
1st row (RS) K3, [wyif sl1 purlwise, k3] to end.
2nd row K1, [wyif sl1 purlwise, k3] to last 2 sts, wyif sl1 purlwise, k1.
These 2 rows form the pattern.

Stitch 022

Bias stockinette stitch LEVEL ❷

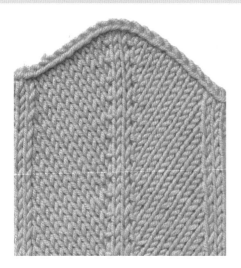

Working regular pairs of increases and decreases tips the stockinette stitch on to the bias and gives the fabric a wavy edge. You can have any number of stitches between the shaping. Space the increases and decreases close together to create chevrons, or place one at each edge for a slanted fabric.

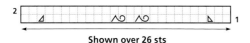

Shown over 26 sts

Specific symbol

🔲 Kfb

Method

1st row (RS) K2, skpo, k7, kfb, k1, kfb, k8, k2tog, k2.
2nd row P.
These 2 rows form the pattern.

Stitch 023

Stars brocade LEVEL ❷

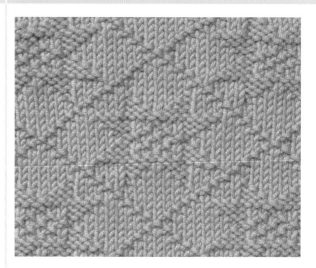

Here, a net of raised stitches is filled in with little eight-pointed stars. It looks complex, but it's all just knit and purl so it's easy to do.

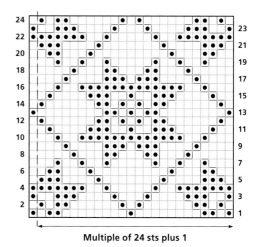

Multiple of 24 sts plus 1

🔲 k on RS, p on WS   ⚫ p on RS, k on WS   ◣ k tbl on RS, p tbl on WS   ◩ k2tog   ◪ skpo

Stitch 024
Embossed hexagons LEVEL ❷

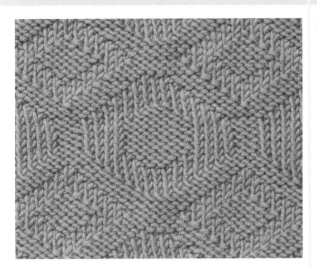

This neat arrangement of knit and purl stitches, with some stitches worked through the back of the loop, is like a patchwork pattern.

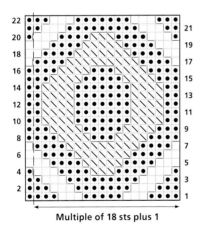

Multiple of 18 sts plus 1

Stitch 025
Embossed pennants LEVEL ❷

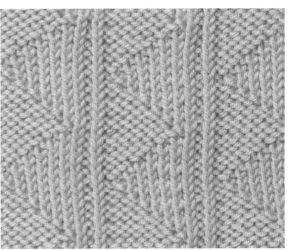

This is the kind of simple stitch pattern that is ideal as a chart because although the patterning changes on both right-side and wrong-side rows, it is easy to see exactly where you are. The contrast between the stitches worked through the back of the loops and the reverse stockinette stitch adds a subtle texture to the pattern.

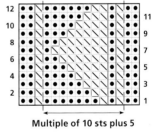

Multiple of 10 sts plus 5

Stitch 026
Corded rib
LEVEL ❷

This interesting variation on a knit two, purl two rib is easy to work and gives a firmly defined texture.

Multiple of
4 sts plus 2

Specific symbol

⌒ Wyab, sl1 purlwise, yo, k1, psso both sts.

Stitch 027
Embossed chevrons
LEVEL ❷

Working the stitches for alternate chevrons through the back of the loops adds definition and gives this simple stitch pattern a sophisticated effect.

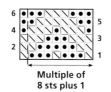

Multiple of
8 sts plus 1

Stitch 028
Brocade net
LEVEL ❷

This subtle arrangement of raised stitches forming a net of diamonds is reminiscent of nineteenth-century whitework bedcovers. Although the other side is not identical, it also has a pretty pattern.

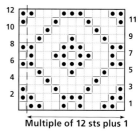

Multiple of 12 sts plus 1

☐ k on RS, p on WS   ● p on RS, k on WS   ⟍ k tbl on RS, p tbl on WS

Stitch 029
Embossed moss diamonds LEVEL ❷

Working alternate stitches in moss stitch through the back of the loops adds to the raised effect. Although the other side is not identical, it is also very pretty, and so the fabric can be reversed.

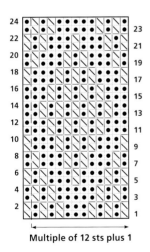

Multiple of 12 sts plus 1

Stitch 030
Flag pleats LEVEL ❷

The slipped stitches emphasize the verticals between the panels of flags. This swatch has been pressed so it lies flat; for a more defined roll to the pleated effect, use a springy pure wool yarn and do not press.

Multiple of 7 sts plus 1

Stitch 031
Little slipped check LEVEL ❷

Alternating slipped stitches between garter ridge rows makes for an interesting raised texture.

Multiple of 4 sts plus 3

Specific symbol
☐ On RS wyab, sl1 purlwise; on WS wyif, sl1 purlwise.

Note
Rows 2–9 form the pattern.

Stitch 032
Five-pointed star
LEVEL ❷

Stitch 033
Plaid weave
LEVEL ❷

A textured motif such as this star shows up clearly against its stockinette-stitch background. Comparing the chart with the knitted motif shows how much seed stitch compresses the row gauge.

Blocks of garter stitch, stockinette stitch, and reverse stockinette stitch make a satisfying stitch pattern with a strongly woven appearance.

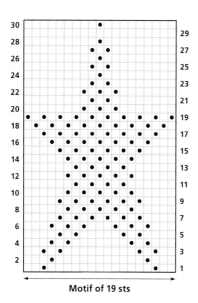

Motif of 19 sts

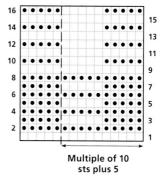

Multiple of 10 sts plus 5

☐ k on RS, p on WS ⬤ p on RS, k on WS ◪ k2tog ◩ skpo ▦ no st ⟲ m1R ⟳ m1L

Stitch 034
Broken rib basketweave
LEVEL ❷

By working wrong-side rows in purl and breaking the rib verticals with groups of purl on the right side, a simple rib becomes an interesting small basketweave design.

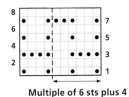

Multiple of 6 sts plus 4

Method
1st row (RS) [P1, k2] to last st, p1.
2nd and WS rows P.
3rd row [P4, k2] to last 4 sts, p4.
5th row As 1st row.
7th row [P1, k2, p3] to last 4 sts, p1, k2, p1.
8th row P.
These 8 rows form the pattern.

Stitch 035
Blackberry stitch
LEVEL ❸

Alternate double increases and decreases on wrong-side rows produce a beautifully regular raised pattern. The right-side rows of purl give the bobbles even more texture.

Multiple of 4 sts

Method
1st row (RS) P.
2nd row [(K1, p1, k1) in 1 st, p3tog] to end.
3rd row P.
4th row [P3tog, (k1, p1, k1) in 1 st] to end.
These 4 rows form the pattern.

Specific symbols
▲ P3tog
Ⅴ (K1, p1, k1) all in 1 st

Stitch 036
Garter stitch chevron
LEVEL ❸

Paired increases and decreases form emphatic chevrons, with garter-stitch ridges underlining the effect. If the bound-off edge is to be as angular as the cast-on edge, the binding off will need to be done on a right-side pattern row and not a knit row.

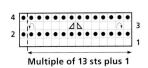

Multiple of 13 sts plus 1

Method
1st row (RS) K.
2nd row K.
3rd row [K1, m1R, k4, skpo, k2tog, k4, m1L] to last st, k1.
4th row K.
Rows 3–4 form the pattern.

STITCH SELECTOR Twists

Crossing stitches without a cable needle is a new-fangled way to make stitches travel. It can bunch them together or send them in diagonals across the knitting's surface. Use twists to draw repeat patterns or to make motifs. The result is like cabling but with a character of its own.

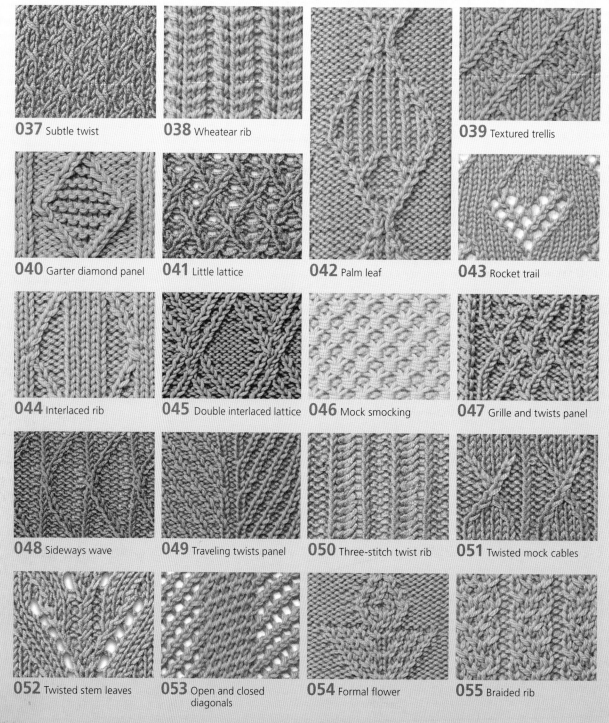

037 Subtle twist

038 Wheatear rib

039 Textured trellis

040 Garter diamond panel

041 Little lattice

042 Palm leaf

043 Rocket trail

044 Interlaced rib

045 Double interlaced lattice

046 Mock smocking

047 Grille and twists panel

048 Sideways wave

049 Traveling twists panel

050 Three-stitch twist rib

051 Twisted mock cables

052 Twisted stem leaves

053 Open and closed diagonals

054 Formal flower

055 Braided rib

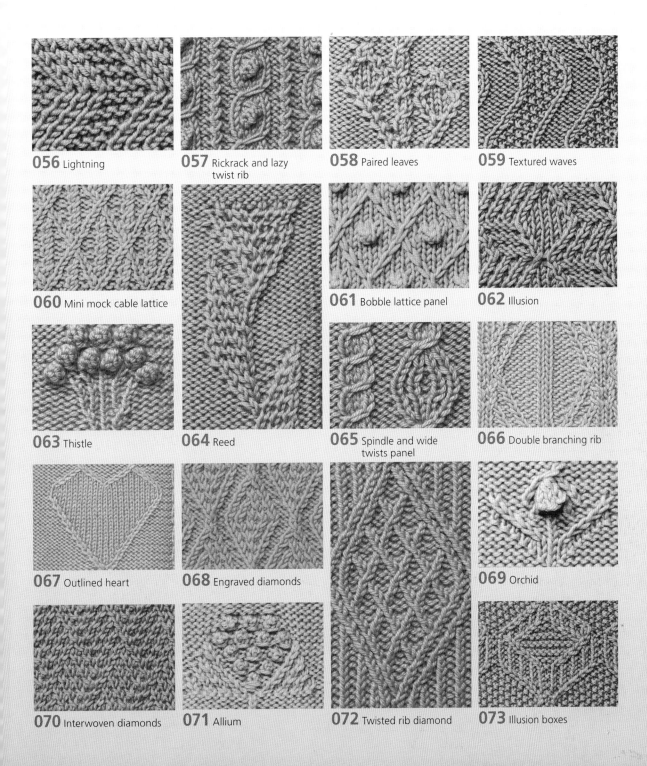

056 Lightning

057 Rickrack and lazy twist rib

058 Paired leaves

059 Textured waves

060 Mini mock cable lattice

061 Bobble lattice panel

062 Illusion

063 Thistle

064 Reed

065 Spindle and wide twists panel

066 Double branching rib

067 Outlined heart

068 Engraved diamonds

069 Orchid

070 Interwoven diamonds

071 Allium

072 Twisted rib diamond

073 Illusion boxes

Stitch 037
Subtle twist
LEVEL ❶

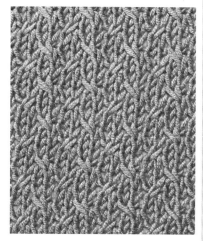

This little pattern with bands of alternating left and right twists is very easy to work. A left twist shows the angle of the top stitch more clearly than a right twist. If you want to compensate for this, pull slightly on the top stitch of each right twist to loosen it.

Multiple of
4 sts plus 4

Method

1st row (RS) K1, [t2L, k2] to last 3 sts, t2L, k1.
2nd row P.
3rd row K1, [k2, t2R] to last 3 sts, k3.
4th row P.
These 4 rows form the pattern.

Stitch 038
Wheatear rib
LEVEL ❶

In this design, left and right twists, separated by a single twisted stitch, make a firm, plump rib that is very stable.

Multiple of
6 sts plus 1

Method

1st row (RS) [P1, t2R, k1 tbl, t2L] to last st, p1.
2nd row K1, [p2, p1 tbl, p2, k1] to end.

Stitch 039
Textured trellis
LEVEL ❶

Half the diamonds in the simple trellis pattern shown here are filled with moss stitch to enrich the surface.

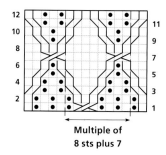

Multiple of
8 sts plus 7

Specific symbol

K tfl of 3rd, 2nd, and 1st sts on L needle; sl all sts tog.

k on RS, p on WS   • p on RS, k on WS   k tbl on RS, p tbl on WS   t2R   t2L   t2Rp   t2Lp

Stitch 040
Garter diamond panel LEVEL ●

Stitch 041
Little lattice LEVEL ●

Stitch 042
Palm leaf LEVEL ●

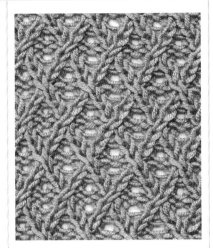

In the above sample, traveling twists outline purl garter-stitch diamonds, giving definition to the stitch pattern.

It is easy to keep your place in this densely patterned stitch, since the direction of the twists changes on every right-side row. On wrong-side rows, knit and purl the stitches as they appear.

Outlined with twist stitches and textured with single twisted rib, this leaf shape makes a panel that could also be used as a repeat pattern.

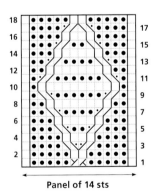

Panel of 14 sts

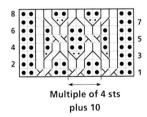

Multiple of 4 sts
plus 10

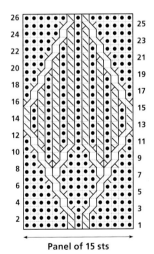

Panel of 15 sts

Method

1st row (RS) P2, [t2R, p2] to end.

2nd row K2, [p2, k2] to end.

3rd row P2, k1, [t2Lp, t2Rp] to last 3 sts, k1, p2.

4th row K2, p1, k1, [p2, k2] to last 6 sts, p2, k1, p1, k2.

5th row P2, k1, p1, [t2L, p2] to last 6 sts, t2L, p1, k1, p2.

6th row As 4th row.

7th row P2, k1, [t2Rp, t2Lp] to last 3 sts, k1, p2.

8th row As 2nd row.

These 8 rows form the pattern.

Stitch 043

Rocket trail LEVEL ❶

Just a few twist stitches
are used in this design to
continue the lines of the
decreases, which form the
eyelets. A single repeat could
easily be used as a panel.

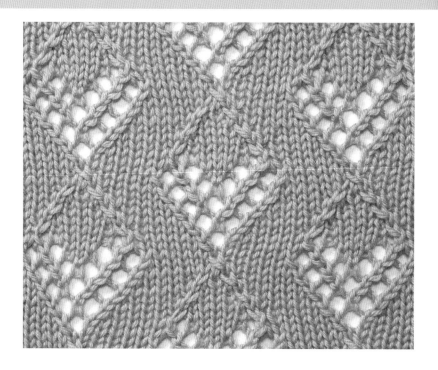

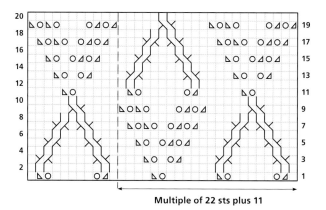

Multiple of 22 sts plus 11

 k on RS, p on WS   p on RS, k on WS k2tog skpo yo t2R t2L t2Rp t2Lp

Stitch 044
Interlaced rib LEVEL ❶

Stitch 045
Double interlaced lattice LEVEL ❶

In this design, wide ribs are linked by long, lazy lines of traveling twist stitches. Use just the sixteen stitches of the repeat for a diamond panel.

Pairs of twists travel under and over to make a large lattice design. You could use the twelve stitches of the repeat with the edge stitches as shown on the chart for a diamond panel.

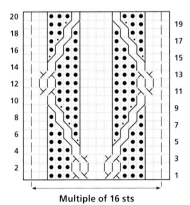

Multiple of 16 sts

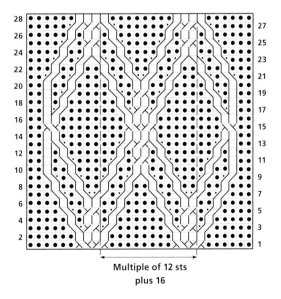

Multiple of 12 sts
plus 16

Stitch 046
Mock smocking LEVEL ❶

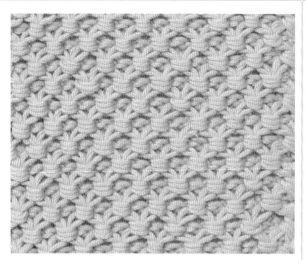

The construction of this stitch pattern is rather like Little lattice (see page 29), but the effect is quite different. Although it's simple to do, this pattern is rather slow to work because of wrapping the yarn around stitches on every wrong-side row.

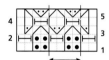

Multiple of 4 sts plus 6

Specific symbol

⊢⊣ [Sl2 purlwise, yf, return sts to L needle, yb] 3 times, sl2 purlwise.

Method

1st row (RS) K2, [p2, k2] to end.
2nd row Cluster 2, [k2, cluster 2] to end.
3rd row K1, [t2Lp, t2Rp] to last st, k1.
4th row P1, k1, cluster 2, [k2, cluster 2] to last 2 sts, k1, p1.
5th row K1, [t2Rp, t2Lp] to last st, k1.

Notes

• When working the cluster, pull firmly on the yarn so the wraps pull the stitches together and lie neatly.
• The 1st row is not repeated, rows 2–5 form the pattern.

Stitch 047
Grille and twists panel LEVEL ❶

Single rib expands and interlaces to make an elegant panel outlined with two-stitch twists. The effect is rich but easy to do, because all the twists are worked on right-side rows.

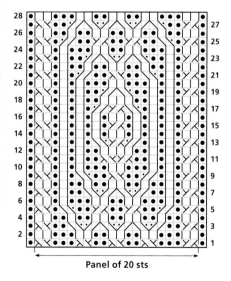

Panel of 20 sts

☐ k on RS, p on WS   ⬛ p on RS, k on WS   ╲ k tbl on RS, p tbl on WS   t2R   t2L   t2Rp   ╲t2Lp

Stitch 048
Sideways wave LEVEL ❶

Single ribs travel, twist around a twisted rib, and return to make this interesting pattern. Work all twenty-one stitches of the chart for a wide panel.

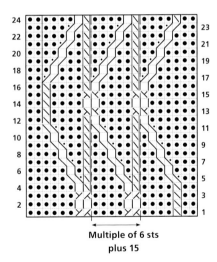

Multiple of 6 sts
plus 15

Stitch 049
Traveling twists panel LEVEL ❶

This stitch pattern gives almost the effect of a cable, but it's easier to work and has a more subtle surface. Here, the left twist and right twist panels are shown next to each other, with each panel worked over eleven stitches, but you could place other stitch patterns between them, or vary the width of the panels. You could even continue the panels over each half of the front of a sweater.

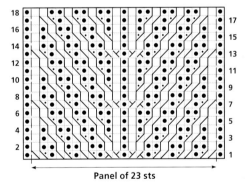

Panel of 23 sts

Stitch 050
Three-stitch twist rib
LEVEL ①

Worked firmly in a springy yarn with relatively small needles, this stitch pattern will pull in like a true rib, but if you choose a flat, floppy yarn and press it flat, the pattern opens out into an interesting striped fabric.

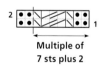

Multiple of 7 sts plus 2

Specific symbol
t3R: On RS k tfl of 3rd st, k tfl of 1st st, k tfl of 2nd st, sl3 tog; on WS p tfl of 2nd st, p tfl of 3rd st, p tfl of 1st st, sl3 tog.

Method
1st row (RS) P2, [k1tbl, t3R, k1tbl, p2] to end.
2nd row K2, [p1tbl, t3R, p1tbl, k2] to end.
These 2 rows form the pattern.

Stitch 051
Twisted mock cables
LEVEL ①

Twists outline ovals of stockinette stitch to give the effect of flat cables. The stitch pattern is given with just a single rib worked through the back of the stitch between the panels, but you could vary the pattern by putting different ribs between or by working more rows straight between the rows with twists.

Method

1st row (RS) P1, [k1 tbl, p3, t2R, p3] to last 2 sts, k1 tbl, p1.
2nd row K1, [p1 tbl, k3, p2, k3] to last 2 sts, p1 tbl, k1.
3rd row P1, [k1 tbl, p2, t2R, t2L, p2] to last 2 sts, k1 tbl, p1.
4th row K1, [p1 tbl, k2, p4, k2] to last 2 sts, p1 tbl, k1.
5th row P1, [k1 tbl, p1, t2R, k2, t2L, p1] to last 2 sts, k1 tbl, p1.
6th and 8th rows K1, [p1 tbl, k1, p6, k1] to last 2 sts, p1 tbl, k1.
7th row P1, [k1tbl, p1, k6, p1] to last 2 sts, k1tbl, p1.
9th row P1, [k1 tbl, p1, t2Lp, k2, t2Rp, p1] to last 2 sts, k1 tbl, p1.
10th row As 4th row.
11th row P1, [k1 tbl, p2, t2Lp, t2Rp, p2] to last 2 sts, k1 tbl, p1.
12th row As 2nd row.
These 12 rows form the pattern.

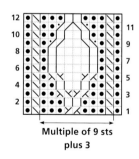

Multiple of 9 sts plus 3

 k on RS, p on WS p on RS, k on WS k tbl on RS, p tbl on WS k2tog skpo yo t2R t2L

Stitch 052
Twisted stem leaves
LEVEL ②

Here, twists add definition to a panel of graceful swirling leaves.

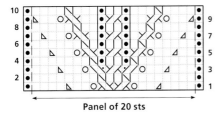

Panel of 20 sts

Stitch 053
Open and closed diagonals
LEVEL ②

Panels of openwork diagonals and twist stitch diagonals flow into each other very smoothly and also form wavy cast-on and cast-off edges.

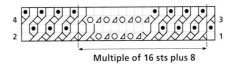

Multiple of 16 sts plus 8

t2Rp   t2Lp

Stitch 054
Formal flower
LEVEL ②

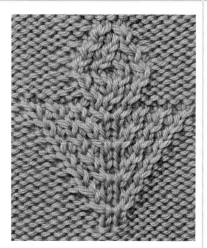

This simple, understated flower can stand alone as a motif, as here, or it could be used as a bold repeat pattern.

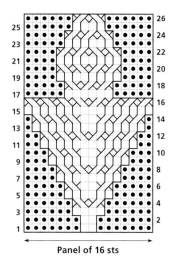

Panel of 16 sts

Note
This design begins on a WS row.

Stitch 055
Braided rib
LEVEL ②

Pairs of twist stitches are arranged to give the illusion of a wide braid. This is a firm, flat rib that doesn't contract.

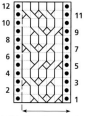

Multiple of 6 sts plus 1

Stitch 056
Lightning
LEVEL ②

Garter-stitch ridges contrast with smooth, sharp zigzags of twist stitches, making a firm, dense fabric.

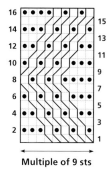

Multiple of 9 sts

☐ k on RS, p on WS   ⬤ p on RS, k on WS   ⟋⟍ t2R   ⟍⟋ t2L

Stitch 057
Rickrack and lazy twist rib
LEVEL 2

This pretty pattern combines two simple elements. The rickrack is made by working a two-stitch twist on every row, and the bobble rib has a five-stitch twist to give the appearance of a cable—but without the work.

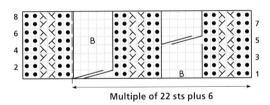

Multiple of 22 sts plus 6

Specific symbols

⊠⊠ On WS insert needle from back between 1st and 2nd sts, catch front strand of 2nd st, pull through to back, p tfl of 2nd st, p tfl of 1st st, sl2 tog.

▱ K tfl of 5th st, k tfl of 1st st, k tfl of 2nd st, k tfl of 3rd st, k tfl of 4th st, sl5 tog.

B (K1, yo, k1, yo, k1) all in 1 st, [turn, k5] twice, lift 4th, 3rd, 2nd, and 1st sts over 5th st and off needle.

Stitch 058
Paired leaves
LEVEL 2

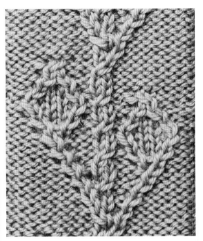

The pairing of these leaves is slightly off-set to give rhythm to a very formal design.

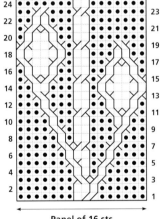

Panel of 16 sts

Stitch 059
Textured waves
LEVEL ②

Alternate panels of seed stitch and reverse stockinette stitch, outlined with neat twist stitches, undulate from side to side. For a single wave in seed stitch, work just the twelve stitches of the repeat.

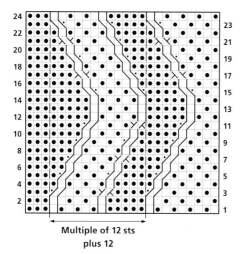

Multiple of 12 sts
plus 12

Stitch 060
Mini mock cable lattice
LEVEL ②

Two-stitch twists form columns of miniature cables framed by a lattice of traveling twists to make a very effective allover pattern.

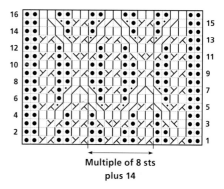

Multiple of 8 sts
plus 14

☐ k on RS, p on WS   ● p on RS, k on WS   t2R   t2L   t2Rp   t2Lp

Stitch 061
Bobble lattice panel
LEVEL ❷

Stitch 062
Illusion
LEVEL ❷

Slipping the traveling stitches on wrong-side rows makes a smooth, well defined lattice, accentuated with neat bobbles, which are actually tiny two-stitch tucks.

Textural stitches and diamonds formed by zigzags give lots of movement to this geometric design.

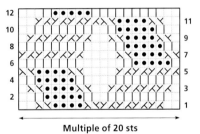

Multiple of 20 sts

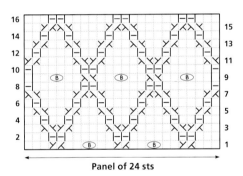

Panel of 24 sts

Specific symbols

⊟ Sl1 purlwise on WS.

◩◪ Insert needle from back between 1st and 2nd sts, catch front of 2nd st, pull through to back, k tfl of 2nd st, k tfl of 1st st, sl2 tog.

◩◪ K tfl of 2nd st, k tfl of 1st st, sl2 tog.

Ⓑ [K2, turn, p2, turn] twice, k each st tog with back loop of corresponding st 4 rows below.

Stitch 063
Thistle
LEVEL ②

Stitch 064
Reed
LEVEL ②

Closely grouped twist stitch diagonals are used here to draw spiky leaves and a stylized seedhead.

Twists, bobbles, and twisted stitches are combined to make a neat little thistle motif. Scatter them in a spot pattern or work them in rows or panels for a textured effect.

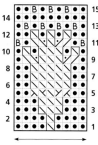

Motif of 9 sts

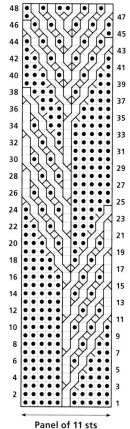

Panel of 11 sts

Specific symbol

B (K1, yo, k1, yo, k1) all in 1 st, turn, [k5, turn] 3 times, [sl1 knitwise] 4 times, k1, pass slipped sts over.

 k on RS, p on WS   p on RS, k on WS k tbl on RS, p tbl on WS   t2R t2Lp   t2L t2Rp

Stitch 065
Spindle and wide twists panel LEVEL ❷

The center motif of this panel alternates between single rib and a four-stitch twist. The cable effect at each side is made by repeating the wide twist.

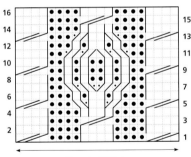

Panel of 20 sts

Specific symbol

K tfl of 4th st, k tfl of 1st st, k tfl of 2nd st, k tfl of 3rd st, sl4 tog.

Stitch 066
Double branching rib LEVEL ❷

In this design, pairs of traveling twist stitches dominate, giving the effect of a diamond lattice linked by two-stitch ribs.

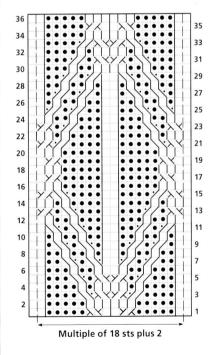

Multiple of 18 sts plus 2

Stitch 067
Outlined heart LEVEL ❸

You can use this motif in lots of ways. Simply place one motif on a reverse-stockinette-stitch background, alternate motifs with stockinette-stitch blocks for a coverlet, or line them up in rows horizontally or vertically to make a panel or a repeat for a garment.

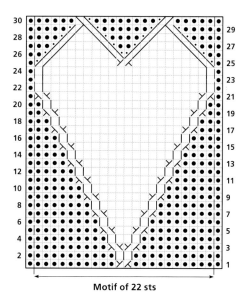

Motif of 22 sts

Specific symbols

⬛ On RS, p tbl of 2nd st, k tfl of 1st st, sl2 tog; on WS, insert R needle from back between 1st and 2nd sts, catch front strand of 2nd st, pull through to back, p tfl of 2nd st, k tfl of 1st st.

⬛ On RS and WS, k tfl of 2nd st, p tfl of 1st st, sl2 tog.

☐ k on RS, p on WS   ⬛ p on RS, k on WS   t2R   t2L   t2Lp   ⬛ t2Rp

Stitch 068
Engraved diamonds LEVEL ③

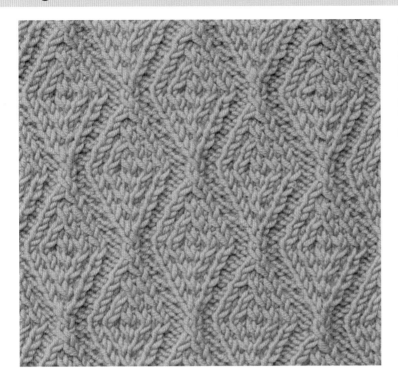

Traveling twist stitches open and close in a diamond shape to reveal another diamond with a twist inside it. The motifs alternate with reverse stockinette stitch to make an allover design. If you want a bold panel, work just the thirty-six stitches as shown on the chart.

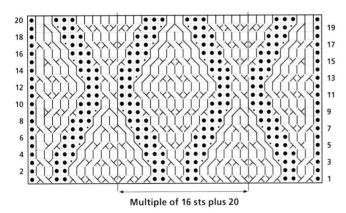

Multiple of 16 sts plus 20

Stitch 069
Orchid
LEVEL ❸

This little motif combines twisted stitches with a bobble to make a pretty flower motif. It can be used alone, stacked up vertically as a panel, or repeated in a spot pattern.

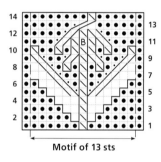

Motif of 13 sts

Specific symbols

⬛ On RS and WS: p tbl of 2nd st, k tfl of 1st st, sl2 tog.

⬛ On RS, k tfl of 2nd st, p tfl of 1st st, sl2 tog; on WS, k tfl of 2nd st, p tbl of 1st st, sl2 tog.

B̲ (K1, yo, k1, yo, k1) all in 1 st, turn, [k5, turn] twice, p5, turn, [sl1 knitwise] 4 times, k1, pass slipped sts over.

⬛ K tfl of 3rd st, p tfl of 1st st, sl this st off L needle then p tfl of 2nd st and sl2 tog.

Stitch 070
Interwoven diamonds
LEVEL ❸

Allover left and right twists in a diamond formation make this a thick, closely textured fabric.

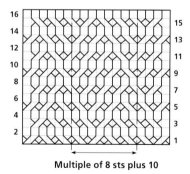

Multiple of 8 sts plus 10

☐ k on RS, p on WS   ⬤ p on RS, k on WS   ◸ k tbl on RS, p tbl on WS   t2R   t2L   t2Rp   ◸◿ t2Lp

Stitch 071
Allium
LEVEL ❸

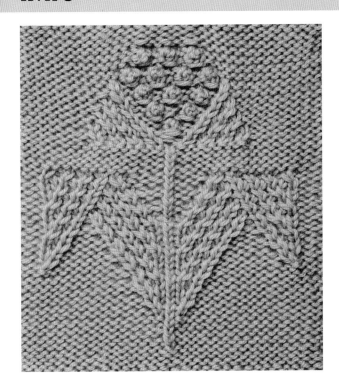

This leaf and flower arrangement of closely worked twist stitches and a single twisted rib has a cluster of small bobbles to suggest the seedhead, and add texture.

Specific symbol

B (K1, p1, k1) all in 1 st, turn, k3, turn, pass 2nd and 3rd sts over 1st st, k tbl.

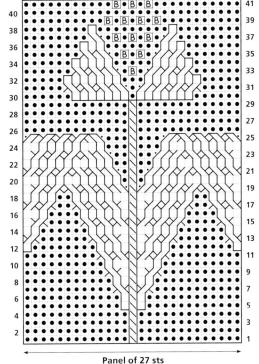

Panel of 27 sts

Stitch 072
Twisted rib diamond LEVEL ❸

There's a double twist to this stitch pattern. The single ribs in the background of the panel are twisted by working into the backs of the stitches, as are the two-stitch twists. Working twisted twists slanting to the left is straightforward, but the right-slanting twisted twists require a cable needle.

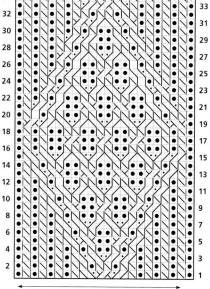

Panel of 20 sts

Specific symbols

⊠⊠ K tbl of 2nd st, k tbl of 1st st, sl2 tog.

⊠⊠ P tbl of 2nd st, k tbl of 1st st, sl2 tog.

⊠⊠ Sl1 to cable needle, hold at back, k1 tbl, then k1 tbl from cable needle.

⊠⊠ Sl1 to cable needle, hold at back, k1 tbl, then p1 tbl from cable needle.

Note

A cable needle is required.

☐ k on RS, p on WS   ● p on RS, k on WS   ⊠ k tbl on RS, p tbl on WS

Stitch 073
Illusion boxes LEVEL ❸

Changes of texture outlined by bands of traveling twisted rib give the effect of looking down into boxes. If you'd like a single, zigzag-textured panel, work just the first to eleventh stitches or the eleventh to twenty-first stitches of the chart.

Specific symbols

On RS, insert R needle from back between 1st and 2nd sts, catch front strand of 2nd st, pull through to back and k tfl of 2nd st, k tfl of 1st st, sl2 tog; on WS, insert needle from back into 2nd st, catch front strand of 2nd st, pull through to back, p tfl of 2nd st, p tfl of 1st st, sl2 tog.

On RS and WS, insert needle from back into 2nd st, catch front strand of 2nd st and pull through to back, p tfl of 2nd st, k tfl of 1st st, sl2 tog.

On RS, k tfl of 2nd st, k tfl of 1st st, sl2 tog; on WS, p tfl of 2nd st, p tfl of 1st st, sl2 tog.

On RS and WS, k tfl of 2nd st, p tfl of 1st st, sl2 tog.

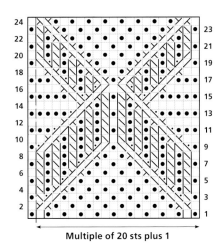

Multiple of 20 sts plus 1

STITCH SELECTOR Cables

Using a cable needle to work groups of stitches out of sequence produces the raised patterns of ropes and braids seen in Aran-style knitting. Start with simple repeats and then graduate to more complex designs before attempting a Celtic knot or a figurative motif.

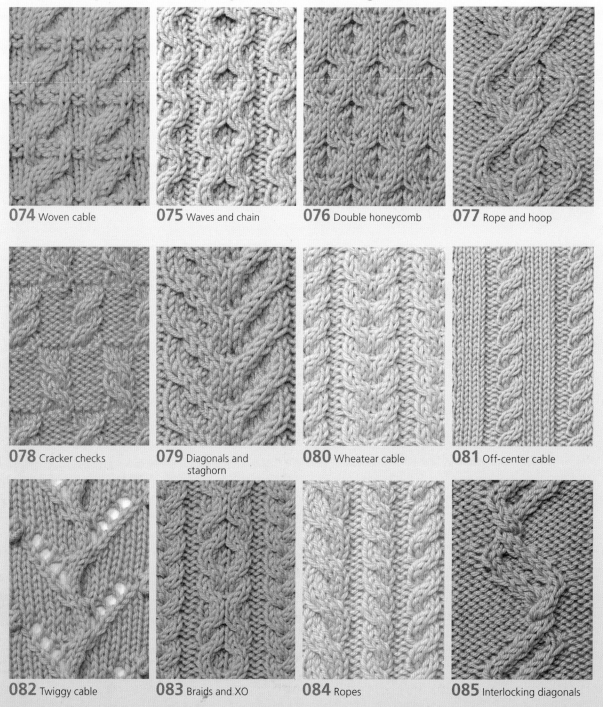

074 Woven cable

075 Waves and chain

076 Double honeycomb

077 Rope and hoop

078 Cracker checks

079 Diagonals and staghorn

080 Wheatear cable

081 Off-center cable

082 Twiggy cable

083 Braids and XO

084 Ropes

085 Interlocking diagonals

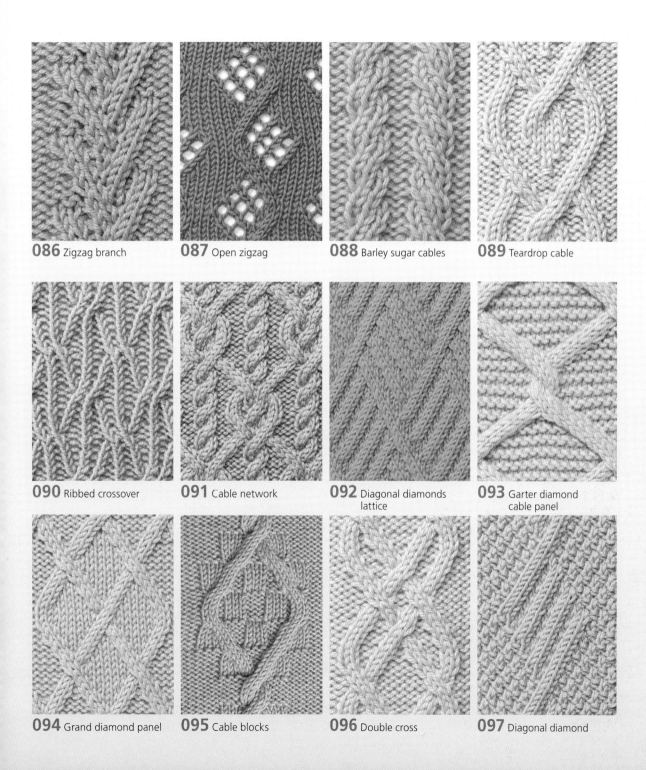

086 Zigzag branch

087 Open zigzag

088 Barley sugar cables

089 Teardrop cable

090 Ribbed crossover

091 Cable network

092 Diagonal diamonds lattice

093 Garter diamond cable panel

094 Grand diamond panel

095 Cable blocks

096 Double cross

097 Diagonal diamond

CABLES—CONTINUED ·

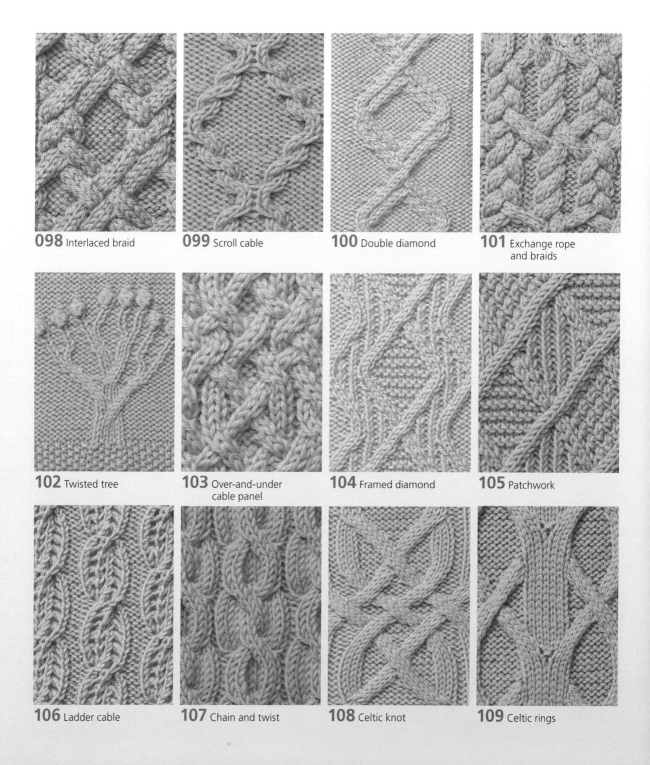

098 Interlaced braid

099 Scroll cable

100 Double diamond

101 Exchange rope and braids

102 Twisted tree

103 Over-and-under cable panel

104 Framed diamond

105 Patchwork

106 Ladder cable

107 Chain and twist

108 Celtic knot

109 Celtic rings

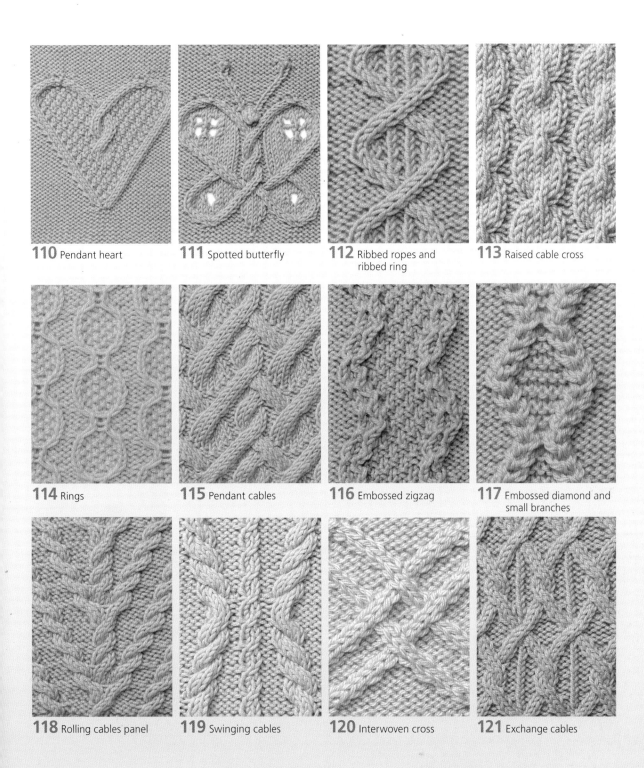

110 Pendant heart

111 Spotted butterfly

112 Ribbed ropes and ribbed ring

113 Raised cable cross

114 Rings

115 Pendant cables

116 Embossed zigzag

117 Embossed diamond and small branches

118 Rolling cables panel

119 Swinging cables

120 Interwoven cross

121 Exchange cables

Stitch 074

Woven cable LEVEL ❶

This six-stitch cable cross is simple enough, but the broken band of reverse stockinette stitch creates an interesting illusion.

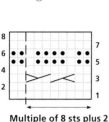

Multiple of 8 sts plus 2

Stitch 075

Waves and chain LEVEL ❶

This is a simple combination of four-stitch cables; single crossings form waves and side-by-side crossings form the central chain.

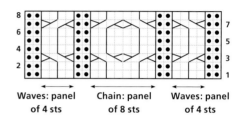

Waves: panel of 4 sts   Chain: panel of 8 sts   Waves: panel of 4 sts

Stitch 076

Double honeycomb LEVEL ❶

Unlike familiar honeycomb stitch formed entirely with four-stitch cable crosses, this version has additional two-stitch crosses for a more dimpled effect.

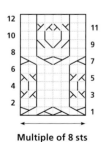

Multiple of 8 sts

Stitch 077

Rope and hoop LEVEL ❶

Basic two-over-two cables are used in this interesting variation on the classic rope design.

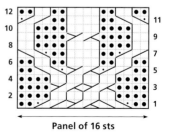

Panel of 16 sts

 k on RS, p on WS   ● p on RS, k on WS   c2b   c2f   c4b   c4f   c4bp

Stitch 078
Cracker checks LEVEL ❶

Little cables, twisted twice to look like crackers, alternate with blocks of reverse stockinette stitch to make this easy-to-work pattern.

Note

Work row 1, repeat rows 2–21 to form the pattern, end the final repeat with row 22.

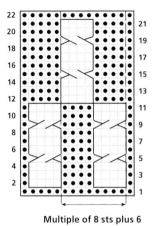

Multiple of 8 sts plus 6

Stitch 079
Diagonals and staghorn LEVEL ❶

Although they consist of only six rows, these gently sloping cables look quite complex. This is the result of repeating the same cable crosses at regular intervals.

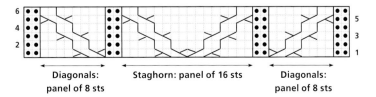

Diagonals:
panel of 8 sts

Staghorn: panel of 16 sts

Diagonals:
panel of 8 sts

c4fp   c6b

Stitch 080
Wheatear cable
LEVEL ❶

Placing two four-stitch cables alongside each other—a back cross followed by a front cross—produces a branching cable. In this swatch, it is used as a repeat pattern.

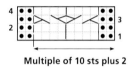

Multiple of 10 sts plus 2

Method
1st row (RS) P2, [k8, p2] to end.
2nd row K2, [p8, k2] to end.
3rd row P2, [c4b, c4f, p2] to end.
4th row As 2nd row.
These 4 rows form the pattern.

Stitch 081
Off-center cable
LEVEL ❶

This design is made over the same number of stitches and rows as wheatear cable, but one cable cross has been dropped and a back cross substituted for a front cross. If this sounds complicated, just look at the chart to see how simple it is.

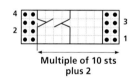

Multiple of 10 sts plus 2

Method
1st row (RS) P2, [k8, p2] to end.
2nd row K2, [p8, k2] to end.
3rd row P2, [k4, c4b, p2] to end.
4th row As 2nd row.
These 4 rows form the pattern.

Stitch 082
Twiggy cable
LEVEL ❶

Although it's set on a stockinette-stitch background, this simple pattern is very well defined. The stem is cabled but the twigs are diagonals of decreases and yarn overs.

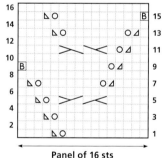

Panel of 16 sts

Specific symbol
B (K1, p1, k1) all in 1 st, turn, p3, turn, sl 2nd and 3rd sts over 1st st, k tbl.

Note
Repeat rows 5–16.

 ☐ k on RS, p on WS   ● p on RS, k on WS   ◸ k2tog   ◺ skpo   O yo   c4b   c4f

Stitch 083
Braids and XO
LEVEL ①

This is an example of the variety that can be achieved with basic four-stitch cables. The firm little braid is only a four-row pattern, whereas the curving XO design requires sixteen rows.

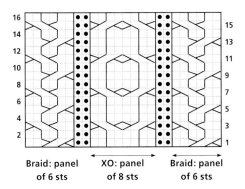

Braid: panel of 6 sts   XO: panel of 8 sts   Braid: panel of 6 sts

Stitch 084
Ropes
LEVEL ①

Repeating the same back or front cross cable at regular intervals makes a classic rope that is substantial enough to stand on its own. It can also be combined with other stitches. Here, the narrow ropes are four-stitch cables, crossing two stitches over two every fourth row, while the wider ropes cross three stitches over three every sixth row.

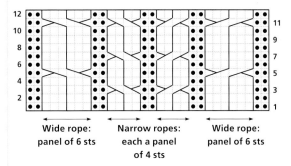

Wide rope: panel of 6 sts   Narrow ropes: each a panel of 4 sts   Wide rope: panel of 6 sts

Method

NARROW ROPE (center right)
1st row (RS) K.
2nd row P.
3rd row C4b.
4th row P.
These 4 rows form the pattern.

NARROW ROPE (center left)
As for center right, but work c4f instead of c4b on 3rd row.

WIDE ROPE (right)
1st and 3rd rows (RS) K.
2nd and 4th rows P.
5th row C6b.
6th row P.
These 6 rows form the pattern.

WIDE ROPE (left)
As for right, but work c6f instead of c6b on 5th row.

c6b   c6f

Stitch 085
Interlocking diagonals LEVEL ②

All these cables are simple two-over-two crossings positioned to make a lively asymmetrical design composed of strong swinging diagonals.

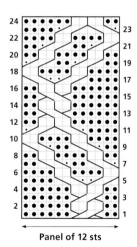

Panel of 12 sts

Stitch 086
Zigzag branch
LEVEL ②

This compact and complex-looking formation of alternating branches is made with only an eight-row pattern repeat.

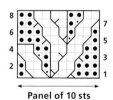

Panel of 10 sts

Stitch 087
Open zigzag
LEVEL ②

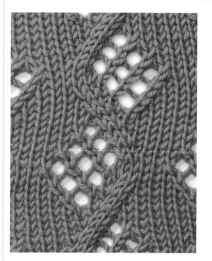

Blocks of lacy texture are tucked into the angles of these zigzag cables to give the stitch additional movement.

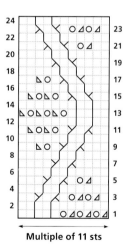

Multiple of 11 sts

 k on RS, p on WS   p on RS, k on WS   k tbl on RS, p tbl on WS   k2tog   skpo   yo   c3b

Stitch 088
Barley sugar cables
LEVEL ②

The spiral effect for these pretty cables is created by crossing three rib stitches over two. Although the stitches are cabled on every fourth row, it takes twelve rows to bring the ribs back to their starting point. You can repeat these cables as shown or use them individually.

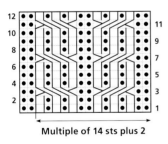

Multiple of 14 sts plus 2

Specific symbols
SI2 to cable needle, hold at back, k1, p1, k1, then p1, k1 from cable needle.

SI3 to cable needle, hold at front, k1, p1, then k1, p1, k1 from cable needle.

Stitch 089
Teardrop cable
LEVEL ②

Cable stitches set on a reverse-stockinette-stitch background are always crisp and well defined. These are softened by the way the central cable cross is set on a group of stitches that form a pendant motif.

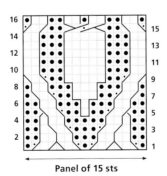

Panel of 15 sts

Specific symbol
SI3 to cable needle, hold at back, k2, sl nearest st from cable needle to L needle, and p st, k rem 2 sts from cable needle.

Stitch 090
Ribbed crossover
LEVEL ②

Five-stitch crosses cause this twisted single rib cable to swing to and fro in a rhythmic way. The wrong side is equally attractive.

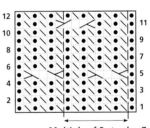

Multiple of 8 sts plus 7

Specific symbols
SI3 to cable needle, hold at front, k1 tbl, p1, work k1 tbl, p1, k1 tbl from cable needle.

SI2 to cable needle, hold at back, k1 tbl, p1, k1 tbl, work p1, k1 tbl from cable needle.

 c3bp c3f c3fp c4b c4f c4bp  c4fp

Stitch 091
Cable network LEVEL ❷

Here's an interesting allover stitch pattern that would also make a bold cable panel. Simply work all the stitches of the chart for a panel.

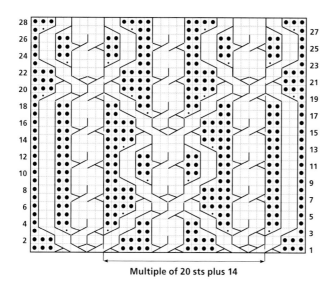

Multiple of 20 sts plus 14

☐ k on RS, p on WS   ● p on RS, k on WS   c3b   c3f   c4b   c4bp

Stitch 092

Diagonal diamonds lattice LEVEL ❷

This exciting, bold, allover pattern is made with just two small cables. It's easier than it looks because every wrong-side row is purl.

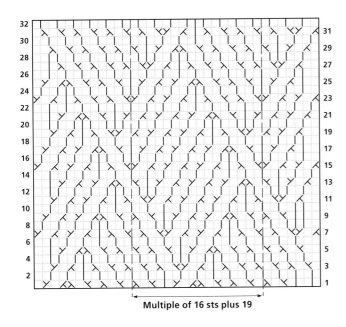

Multiple of 16 sts plus 19

c4f   c4fp

Stitch 093
Garter diamond cable panel LEVEL ❷

This richly textured cable panel looks intricate, but in fact it's easy to work because every wrong-side row is just purl.

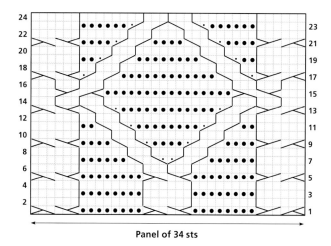

Panel of 34 sts

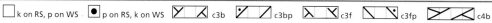

☐ k on RS, p on WS   ● p on RS, k on WS   c3b   c3bp   c3f   c3fp   c4b

Stitch 094
Grand diamond panel LEVEL ❷

The center cable opens up to make a diamond with a stockinette-stitch background crossed by the traveling stitches from the cables at each side. The effect is both refined and bold.

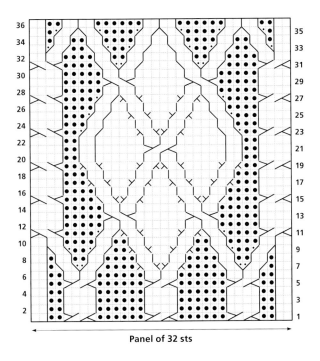

Panel of 32 sts

c4f   c5bp   c5fp   c6b   c6f

Stitch 095
Cable blocks
LEVEL ❷

Blocks of stockinette stitch checker this bold diamond panel and extend into the background of reverse stockinette stitch.

Specific symbol

⬡ Sl6 to cable needle, hold at back, k3, sl nearest 3 sts from cable needle to L needle, p3, k3 rem sts from cable needle.

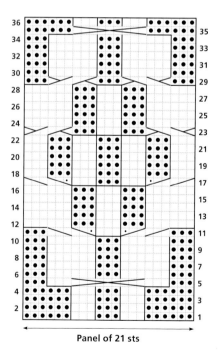

Panel of 21 sts

Stitch 096
Double cross
LEVEL ❷

Two types of cables are used here to make gentle interlacings, but both are simple and follow a very logical progression.

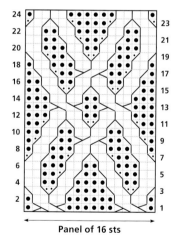

Panel of 16 sts

☐ k on RS, p on WS   ⬛ p on RS, k on WS   ⟋⟍ c3b   ⟋⟋ c3bp   ⟍⟍ c3fp   ⟋⟍ c4b

⟋⟍⟋ c6f   ⟍⟍⟍ c6fp

Stitch 097
Diagonal diamond
LEVEL ②

Stitch 098
Interlaced braid
LEVEL ②

Closely positioned four-stitch cables on a background of moss stitch make a simple but richly textured design.

Here's a really satisfying cable panel that interlocks eight strands to make a rich braid.

Panel of 36 sts

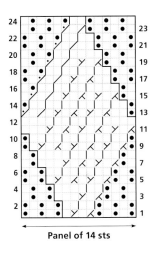

Panel of 14 sts

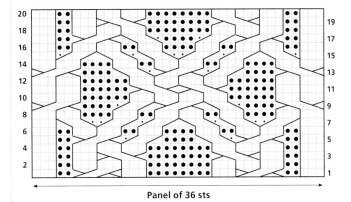 c4f c5bp c5fp c6b c6bp

Stitch 099
Scroll cable LEVEL ❷

These curvy ropes are made to swing by being cabled over six stitches. The result is a very elegant diamond design.

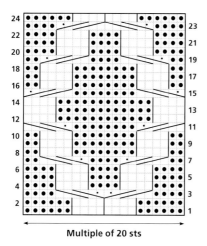

Multiple of 20 sts

Specific symbols

Sl4 to cable needle, hold at back, k2, then k2, p2 from cable needle.

Sl2 to cable needle, hold at front, p2, k2, then k2 from cable needle.

Stitch 100
Double diamond LEVEL ❷

Parallel sets of cables give this design structural stability and create a pleasing under-and-over visual pattern.

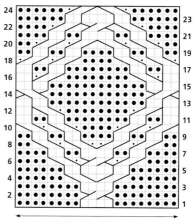

Panel of 20 sts

k on RS, p on WS   ● p on RS, k on WS   c4b   c4bp   c4f   c4fp

Stitch 101
Exchange rope and braids LEVEL ❷

This really satisfying, busy cable panel is made up of two simple elements: a rope cable in the center linked to braided cables at each side. Although the row repeat is quite short, the effect is complex.

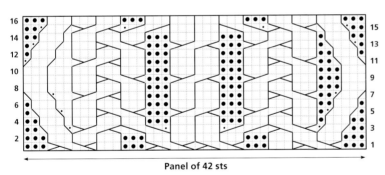

Panel of 42 sts

Specific symbols

⟋ Sl1 to cable needle, hold at back, k3, then p1 from cable needle.

⟍ Sl3 to cable needle, hold at front, p1, then k3 from cable needle.

Stitch 102

Twisted tree

LEVEL ❷

Cables branch out from a center trunk to make a tree finished with nubbly bobbles.

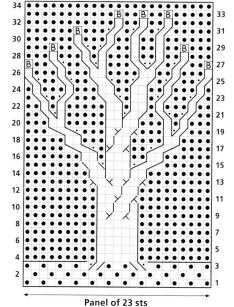

Panel of 23 sts

Specific symbol

B (K1, yo, k1, yo, k1) all in 1 st, turn, p5, turn, [sl1 knitwise] 4 times, k1, pass slipped sts over.

☐ k on RS, p on WS   ● p on RS, k on WS   ◣ k tbl on RS, p tbl on WS   ◥◥ c2fp   ◿◿ c2bp   ⅄ ◸ c3b

Stitch 103
Over-and-under cable panel
LEVEL ❷

As you work more repeats of this panel, you'll see long diagonal over-and-under strands appear as well as the more obvious center cross. Although the effect is complex, the panel is made with just four simple cables.

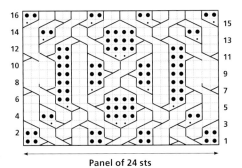

Panel of 24 sts

Stitch 104
Framed diamond
LEVEL ❷

In this design, simple diamonds outlined with zigzags have garter stitch and twisted rib added for a richly textured effect.

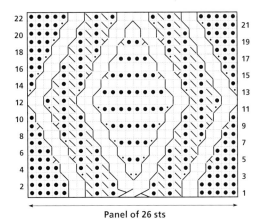

Panel of 26 sts

c3bp   c3f   c3fp   c4b   c4bp   c4f   c4fp

Stitch 105
Patchwork LEVEL ❷

Alternating the texture stitches that fill the outside diamonds of this panel gives the impression of a varied patchwork rather than a regular repeat.

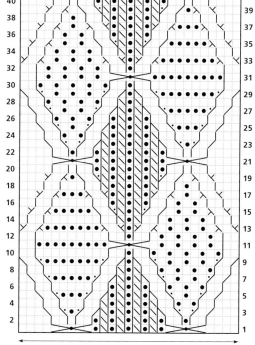

Panel of 27 sts

Specific symbol

Sl3 to cable needle, hold at back, k2, sl nearest st from cable needle back to L needle, and p st, then k2 from cable needle.

 k on RS, p on WS   ● p on RS, k on WS   ╲ k tbl on RS, p tbl on WS   ╱ k2tog   ╲ skpo   O yo   c3b

Stitch 106
Ladder cable LEVEL ②

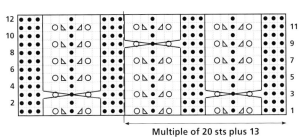

Multiple of 20 sts plus 13

Lacy ladders help define this cable stitch and also give the fabric a light, airy quality that's unusual in a cable stitch.

Specific symbol

Sl4 to cable needle, hold at back, k1, yo, k2tog, sl nearest st from cable needle to L needle and p st, then skpo, yo, k1 from cable needle.

Stitch 107
Chain and twist LEVEL ②

Crossing three stitches over three gives this cable-stitch pattern its roundness and definition.

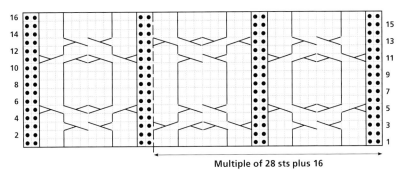

Multiple of 28 sts plus 16

c3bp   c3f   c3fp   c6b   c6f

Stitch 108

Celtic knot LEVEL ❸

Here, hidden increases and decreases give the illusion of a continuous line to make this Celtic knot design.

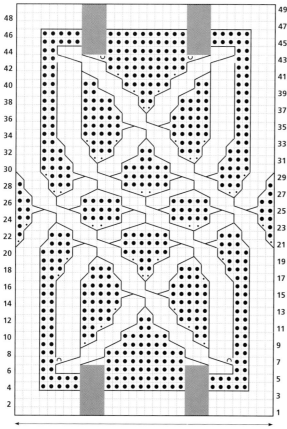

Motif of 26 sts, with a variable stitch count

Specific symbols

Sl1 to cable needle, hold at back, k3, then p1 from cable needle.

Sl3 to cable needle, hold at front, p1, then k3 from cable needle.

Insert cable needle into top of each of next 3 sts in row below, hold at back, k3, then k3 from cable needle.

K into top of each of next 3 sts in row below, then k next 3 sts on L needle.

Sl3 to cable needle, hold at back, [k next st tog with next st on cable needle] 3 times.

Sl3 to cable needle, hold at front, [k next st on cable needle tog with next st on L needle] 3 times.

 k on RS, p on WS   • p on RS, k on WS   k3tog   no st   c5bp   c5fp

Stitch 109
Celtic rings LEVEL ❸

Specific symbols

⬚ Sl1 to cable needle, hold at back, k3, then k1 from cable needle.

⬚ Sl3 to cable needle, hold at front, k1, then k3 from cable needle.

⬚ Sl1 to cable needle, hold at back, k3, then p1 from cable needle.

⬚ Sl3 to cable needle, hold at front, p1, then k3 from cable needle.

⬚ Sl 1st st knitwise, sl 2nd st knitwise, k1, pass slipped sts over.

⬚ Work m1R and m1L into same strand between sts.

This design is based on a carved stone border pattern and uses curved cables that branch out from the center and overlap to make interlocking rings.

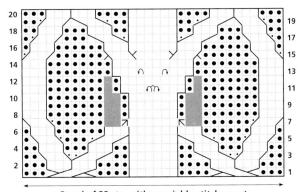

Panel of 32 sts, with a variable stitch count

c6b   c6bp   c6f   c6fp   m1R   m1L

Stitch 110
Pendant heart LEVEL ❸

Apart from the multiple increase at the beginning and the multiple decreases on the last row, this motif combines just a few techniques to produce a striking effect.

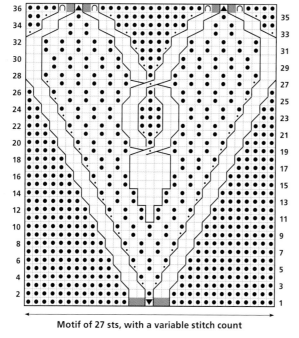

Motif of 27 sts, with a variable stitch count

Specific symbols

▼ M1, in next st k1 tbl then k tfl, insert point of L needle behind vertical strand between 2 sts just made and k tbl, m1.

▲ Wyif, sl3 to R needle, * on R needle sl 2nd st over 1st st, sl this st back to L needle, sl 2nd st over it, ** sl this st back to R needle; rep from * to ** once more, leaving 1 st on L needle; wyab, k this st.

⬚⬚⬚ Sl3 to cable needle, hold at back, k2, sl nearest st from cable needle to L needle, p this st, then k2 rem sts from cable needle.

∩ M1 on WS.

☐ k on RS, p on WS   ● p on RS, k on WS   k2tog   skpo   p2tog   sk2po   yo   ▨ no st   c2fp

∩ m1R   ∩ m1L

Stitch 111
Spotted butterfly LEVEL ❸

A butterfly can be created by combining cables with a few other techniques. All the stitches are quite straightforward; it's just the mixture that makes this design rather complex.

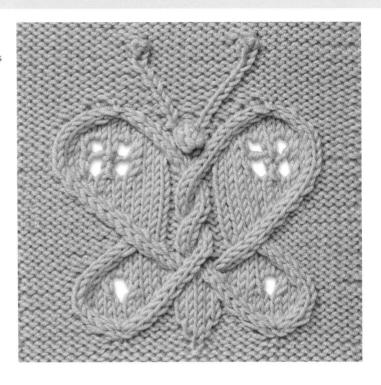

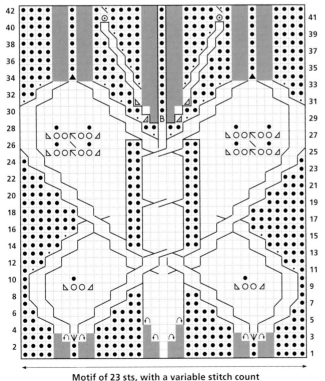

Motif of 23 sts, with a variable stitch count

Specific symbols

Ⓑ (K1, yo, k1, yo, k1) all in 1 st, turn, p5, turn, k5, turn, p2tog, p1, p2tog, turn, s2kpo.

⊙ (K1, yo, k1) all in 1 st, turn, k3, turn, sk2po

⩗ K1 tbl on WS.

⩘ P tbl on WS.

∩ M1 on WS

Ⓥ (K1 tbl, k1) all in 1 st, insert L needle in strand between sts just made and k1 tbl of strand to make 3 sts from 1.

▲ Wyif sl3 to R needle, * on R needle sl 2nd st over 1st st, sl this st back to L needle, sl 2nd st over it; ** sl this st back to R needle; rep from * to ** once more, leaving 1 st on L needle; wyab, k this st.

⬎⬍ Sl3 to cable needle, hold at back, k2, sl nearest st from cable needle to L needle, k this st tbl, then k2 rem sts from cable needle.

c2bp | c3b | c3bp | c3f | c3fp | c4b | c4bp | c4f | c4fp

Stitch 112

Ribbed ropes and ribbed ring LEVEL 3

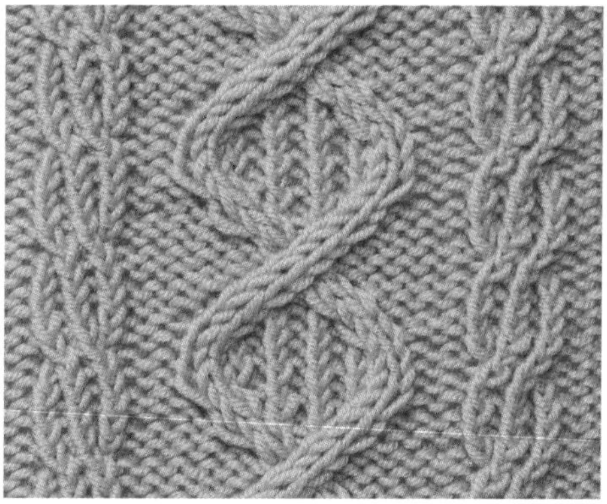

Crossing three stitches of twisted rib over two stitches makes a gently curving rope, while the same twisted rib is used to fill the almost circular cable.

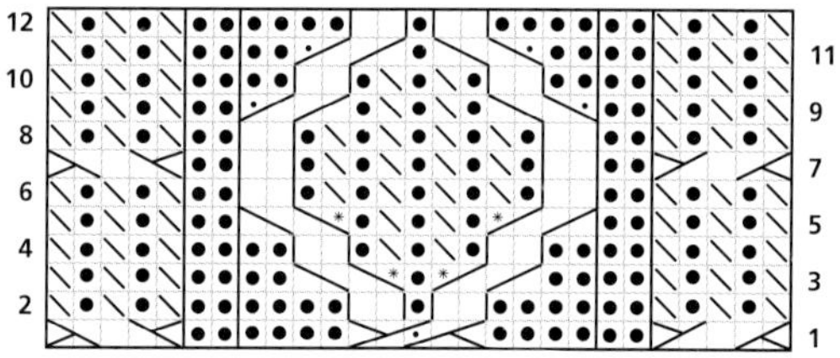

Ribbed rope: panel of 5 sts — Ribbed ring: panel of 13 sts — Ribbed rope: panel of 5 sts

Specific symbols

Sl2 to cable needle, hold at back, k1 tbl, p1, k1 tbl, then p1, k1 tbl from cable needle.

Sl3 to cable needle, hold at front, k1 tbl, p1, then k1 tbl, p1, k1 tbl from cable needle.

Sl3 to cable needle, hold at back, k2, sl nearest st from cable needle to L needle, p this st, then k2 rem sts from cable needle.

Sl2 to cable needle, hold at back, k2, then p1, k1 tbl from cable needle.

Sl2 to cable needle, hold at front, k1 tbl, p1, then k2 from cable needle.

Stitch 113

Raised cable cross LEVEL 3

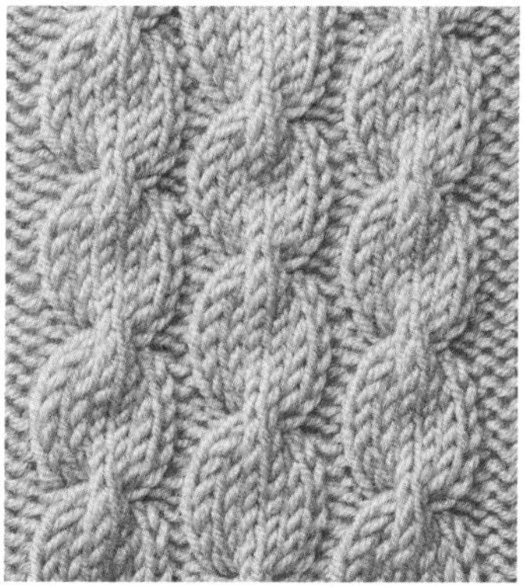

This method of using two cable needles to cross six stitches produces the effect of a very three-dimensional but very soft chain.

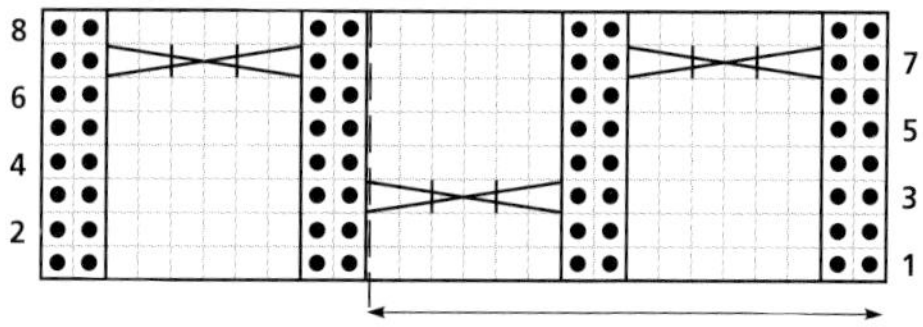

Multiple of 16 sts plus 10

Specific symbol

Sl2 to 1st cable needle, hold at back, sl2 to 2nd cable needle, hold at front, k2, then k2 from 2nd cable needle, then k2 from 1st cable needle.

Note

Two cable needles are required.

k on RS, p on WS | p on RS, k on WS | k tb1 on RS, p tb1 on WS | c5bp | c5fp

Stitch 114
Rings LEVEL ❸

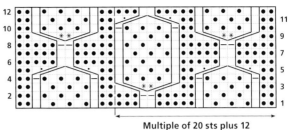

Multiple of 20 sts plus 12

A circular cable is achieved by slipping the stitch on the previous row that is to be carried across on the right side. The center of the ring is textured with seed stitch.

Specific symbols

⊟ Wyif, sl1 purlwise on WS.

Sl3 to cable needle, hold at back, k1, then p1, k1, p1 from cable needle.

Sl1 to cable needle, hold at front, k1, p1, k1, then k1 from cable needle.

Sl3 to cable needle, hold at back, k1, then p3 from cable needle.

Sl1 to cable needle, hold at front, p3, then k1 from cable needle.

Stitch 115
Pendant cables LEVEL ❸

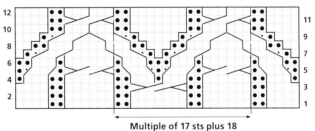

Multiple of 17 sts plus 18

Two or three repeats of this pattern, plus the edge stitches, makes a bold cable panel. If you want to work a mirror image of this pattern, cross the six-stitch and seven-stitch cables the opposite way.

Specific symbols

Sl1 to cable needle, hold at back, k3, then p1 from cable needle.

Sl3 to cable needle, hold at front, p1, then k3 from cable needle.

Sl4 to cable needle, hold at back, k3, sl end st from cable needle to L needle, hold cable needle at front, p1, then k3 rem sts from cable needle.

 c6b

Stitch 116
Embossed zigzag
LEVEL **3**

Stitch 117
Embossed diamond and small branches LEVEL **3**

Cables embellished with a honeycomb of twist stitches and separated by a panel of moss stitch add up to an unusual and richly textured design.

The texture of both these panels depends on a single traveling stitch. For the embossed diamond, two sets of twist stitches are worked as part of the cable, whereas in small branches the crossed stitches are all cabled.

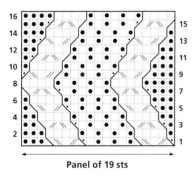

Panel of 19 sts

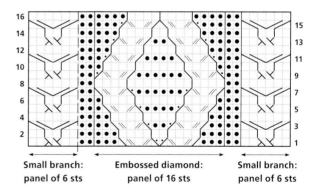

Small branch: panel of 6 sts **Embossed diamond: panel of 16 sts** **Small branch: panel of 6 sts**

Specific symbols

SI4 to cable needle, hold at front, p1, then t2R, t2L from cable needle.

SI4 to cable needle, hold at front, p1, then t2L, t2R from cable needle.

SI1 to cable needle, hold at back, t2R, t2L, then p1 from cable needle.

SI1 to cable needle, hold at back, t2L, t2R, then p1 from cable needle.

Specific symbols

SI2 to cable needle, hold at back, k1, then k2 from cable needle.

SI1 to cable needle, hold at front, k2, then k1 from cable needle.

SI1 to cable needle, hold at back, t2R, t2L, then p1 from cable needle.

SI4 to cable needle, hold at front, p1, then t2R, t2L from cable needle.

 k on RS, p on WS   p on RS, k on WS   c2b   c2f   c4b   c4f

Stitch 118
Rolling cables panel
LEVEL ❸

Although the traveling cables look like four-stitch ropes, they take in two of the background stitches each time, so they travel outward to give a decorative chevron.

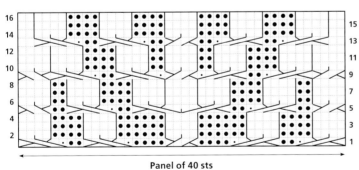

Panel of 40 sts

Specific symbols

Sl4 to cable needle, hold at back, k2, then k4 from cable needle.

Sl4 to cable needle, hold at back, k2, then k2, p2 from cable needle.

Sl2 to cable needle, hold at front, k4, then k2 from cable needle.

Sl2 to cable needle, hold at front, p2, k2, then k2 from cable needle.

Stitch 119
Swinging cables LEVEL ❸

Taking one extra stitch in from the background each time you cable makes the cabled rope travel gently from side to side. You'll need two cable needles to work the tiny rib cables that edge and divide the panel.

Specific symbols

⬚⬚ Sl2 to cable needle, hold at back, k1, sl nearest st from cable needle to L needle, hold cable needle at front, p1, then k1 from cable needle.

⬚⬚ Sl1 to 1st cable needle, hold at front, sl next st on to 2nd cable needle, hold at back, k1, p1 from 2nd cable needle, then k1 from 1st cable needle.

⬚⬚ Sl4 to cable needle, hold at back, k3, then k3, p1 from cable needle.

⬚⬚ Sl3 to cable needle, hold at front, p1, k3, then k3 from cable needle.

Note

Two cable needles are required.

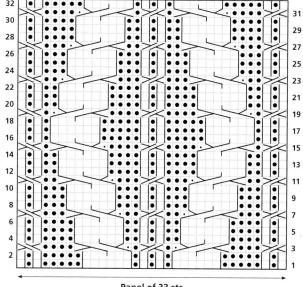

Panel of 33 sts.

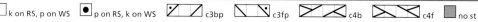 ☐ k on RS, p on WS ● p on RS, k on WS   c3bp   c3fp   c4b   c4f ▨ no st

Stitch 120
Interwoven cross LEVEL ❸

The simple geometry of this motif is very satisfying. The cable crosses are quite basic; only the multiple increases and decreases are unusual features.

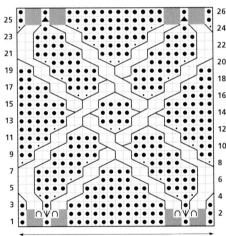

Motif of 16 sts, with a variable stitch count

Specific symbols

Ⅴ (K1 tbl, k1) all in 1 st, insert L needle behind vertical strand between 2 sts just made, k1 tbl of strand to make 3 sts from 1.

▲ Wyif, sl3 to R needle, * on R needle sl 2nd st over 1st, sl this st back to needle, sl 2nd st over it, ** sl this st back to R needle; rep from * to ** once more, leaving 1 st on L needle; wyab k this st.

Note

This design begins on a wrong-side row.

Stitch 121
Exchange cables LEVEL ❸

Rope cables divide and interlace to make a lattice over neatly defined verticals of twisted rib. To turn this allover pattern into a bold panel, work three repeats plus the edge stitches.

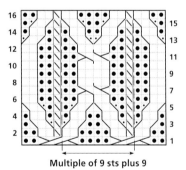

Multiple of 9 sts plus 9

Specific symbol

▷◁ Sl3 to cable needle, hold at back, k2, sl nearest st on cable needle to L needle, hold cable needle at front, k1 tbl, then k2 from cable needle.

 m1   c4bp  c4fp ⃠ k tbl on RS, p tbl on WS

STITCH SELECTOR Lace

The effects that you can achieve with lace stitches vary from bold outlines to ethereal allover patterns, but the principle is always the same, with open yarn-over increases balanced by some type of decrease. Lace patterns also combine well with raised texture stitches.

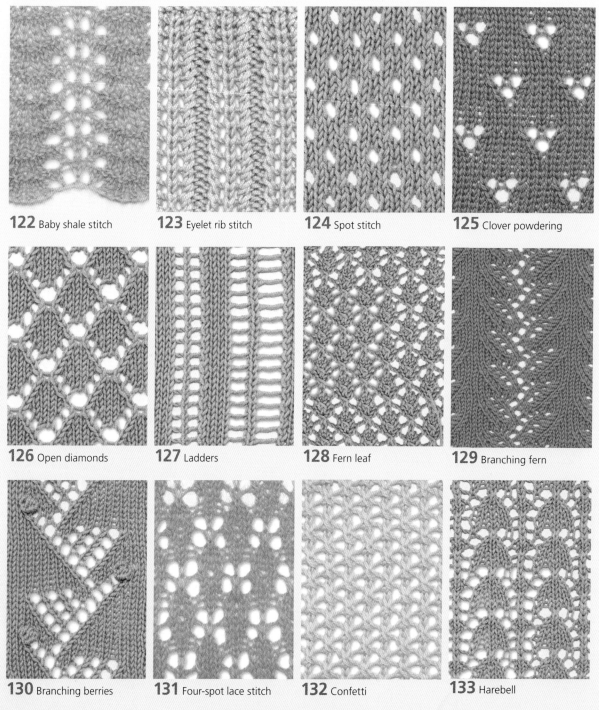

122 Baby shale stitch

123 Eyelet rib stitch

124 Spot stitch

125 Clover powdering

126 Open diamonds

127 Ladders

128 Fern leaf

129 Branching fern

130 Branching berries

131 Four-spot lace stitch

132 Confetti

133 Harebell

134 Little rose lace stitch

135 Little fan stitch

136 Zigzag lace

137 Chevron lace

138 Daisy and ladder

139 Crocus stitch

140 Jeweled heart

141 Bird's eye

142 Lacy paisley

143 Trellis and vine

144 Moon flower

LACE—CONTINUED

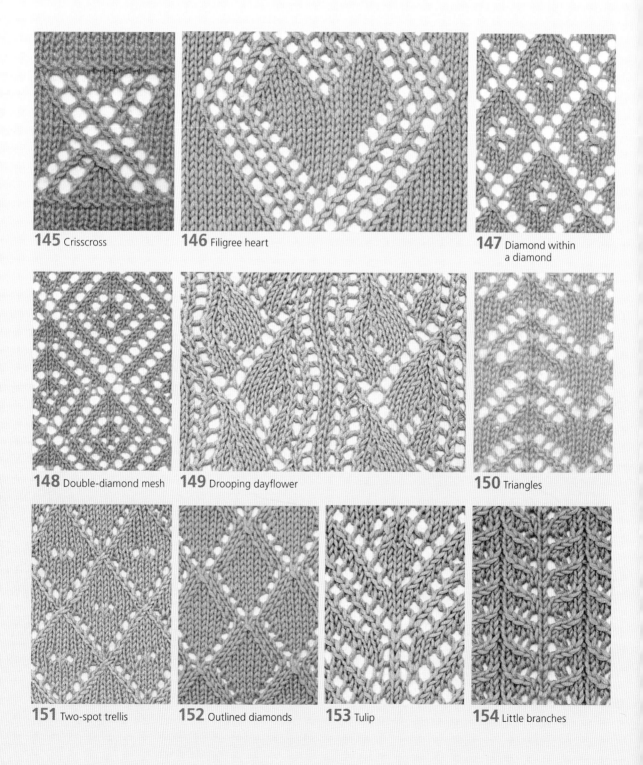

145 Crisscross

146 Filigree heart

147 Diamond within a diamond

148 Double-diamond mesh

149 Drooping dayflower

150 Triangles

151 Two-spot trellis

152 Outlined diamonds

153 Tulip

154 Little branches

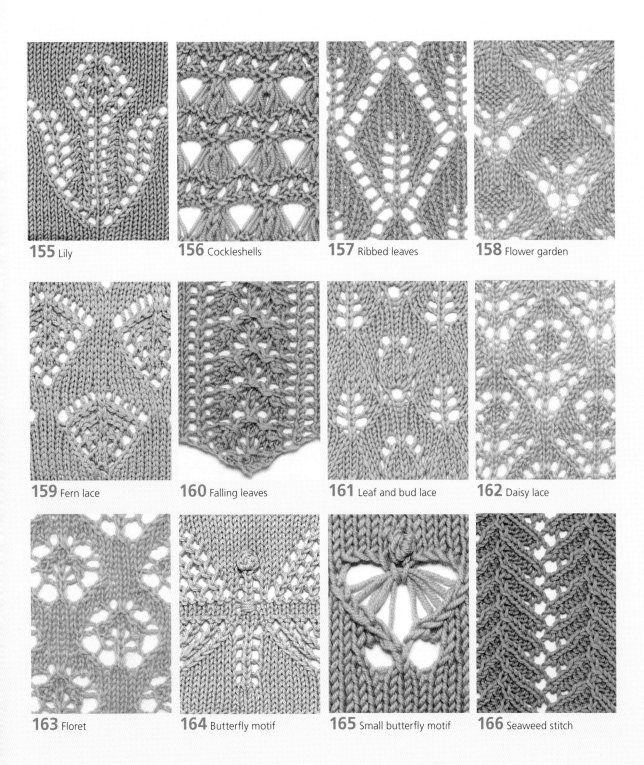

155 Lily

156 Cockleshells

157 Ribbed leaves

158 Flower garden

159 Fern lace

160 Falling leaves

161 Leaf and bud lace

162 Daisy lace

163 Floret

164 Butterfly motif

165 Small butterfly motif

166 Seaweed stitch

Stitch 122

Baby shale stitch LEVEL 1

Groups of decreases and yarn-over increases alternate to give a gracefully undulating design that's the smallest version possible of the traditional old shale-stitch pattern.

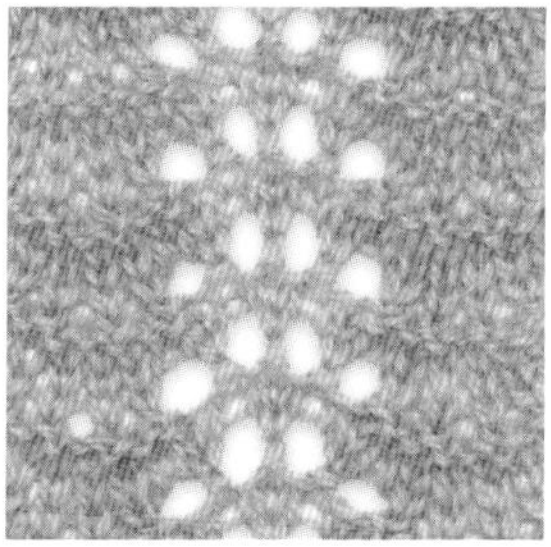

Method

1st row (RS) K1, * [k2tog] twice, [yo, k1] 3 times, yo, [skpo] twice, rep from * to last st, k1.

2nd row P.

3rd row K.

4th row K.

These 4 rows form the pattern.

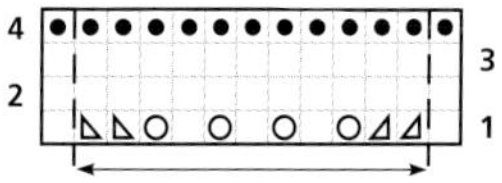

Multiple of 11 sts plus 2

Stitch 123

Eyelet rib stitch LEVEL 1

Paired decreases and yarn overs are stacked up closely and alternated with a purl stitch to make an openwork rib.

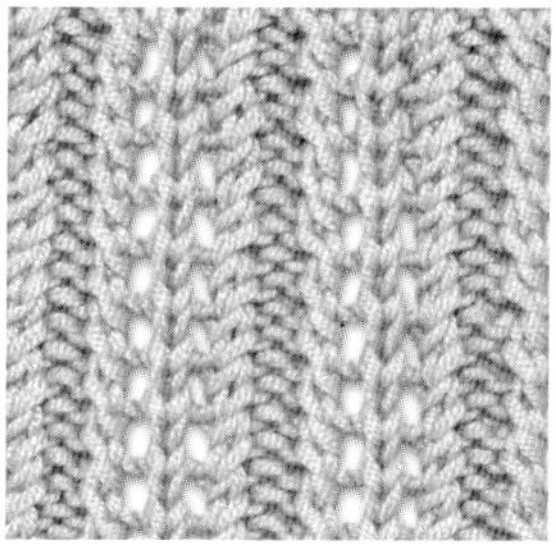

Method

1st row (RS) [P1, k2tog, yo, k1, yo, skpo] to last st, p1.

2nd row [K1, p5] to last st, k1.

These 2 rows form the pattern.

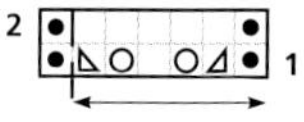

Multiple of 6 sts plus 1

Stitch 124

Spot stitch LEVEL 1

This is the simplest kind of lace—just rows of holes arranged in a spot pattern—but what makes this variation different is that the holes are made alternately on right-side and wrong-side rows.

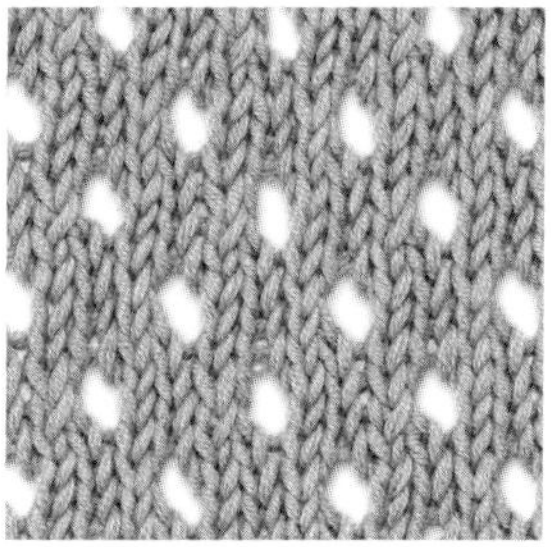

Method

1st row (RS) K.

2nd row P.

3rd row K2, [yo, k2tog, k2] to last 3 sts, yo, k2tog, k1.

4th row P.

5th row K.

6th row P3, [p2tog, yo, p2] to last 2 sts, p2.

These 6 rows form the pattern.

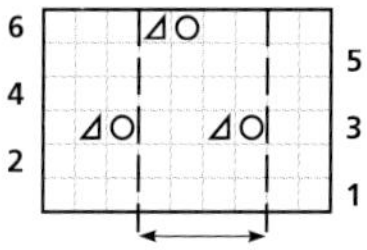

Multiple of 4 sts plus 5

Specific symbol

◿ K2tog on RS rows, p2tog on WS rows.

Stitch 125

Clover powdering LEVEL 1

The charm of this small half-drop pattern is its utter simplicity. The flowers almost quilt the surface of the stockinette stitch.

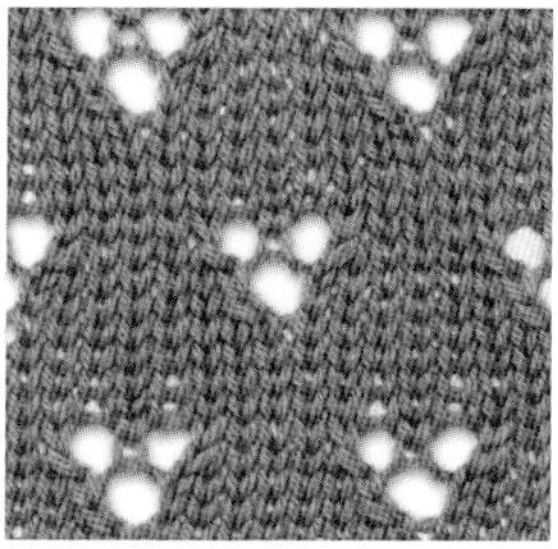

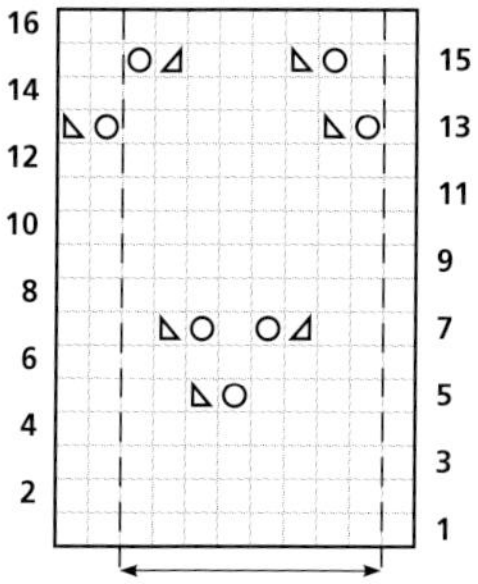

Multiple of 8 sts plus 3

□ k on RS, p on WS ● p on RS, k on WS ⧅ k tbl on RS, p tbl on WS ◿ k2tog ◺ skpo Λ s2kpo ⋀ sk2po ○ yo

Stitch 126
Open diamonds LEVEL ❶

At the base of these open diamonds is a double yarn over, which punctuates the design and causes the decrease-stitch outlines to curve gently.

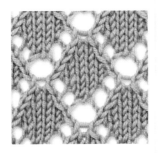

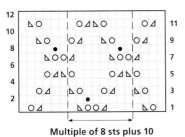

Multiple of 8 sts plus 10

Stitch 127
Ladders LEVEL ❶

Lace ladders have an attractive simplicity and they can be used to outline panels of other stitches, or either panel can be used as a repeat.

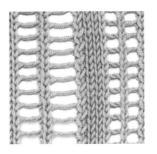

Wide ladder: panel of 9 sts

Narrow ladder: panel of 7 sts

Method

1st row (RS) K1, skpo, yo twice, s2kpo, yo twice, k2tog, k1.
2nd row P2, k1, p2 ,k1, p3. These 2 rows form the pattern.

Method

1st row (RS) K1, skpo, yo, k1 tbl, yo, k2tog, k1.
2nd row P3, p1 tbl, p3. These 2 rows form the pattern.

Stitch 128
Fern leaf LEVEL ❶

Tiny leaves mesh together to make a very regular allover lace pattern. Except at the side edges, all the decreases are double decreases.

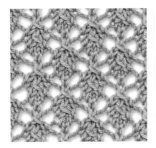

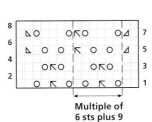

Multiple of 6 sts plus 9

Stitch 129
Branching fern LEVEL ❶

The graceful curves of this stitch pattern make it look more complex than it really is. The effect is created by the positioning of the yarn overs in relation to the decreases.

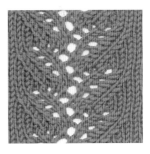

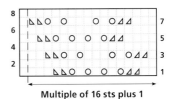

Multiple of 16 sts plus 1

Stitch 130
Branching berries
LEVEL ❶

Single bobbles accentuate the asymmetrical character of this zigzag design.

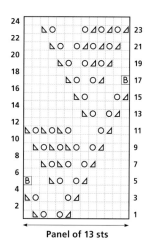

Panel of 13 sts

Specific symbol
B (K1, p1, k1, p1, k1) all in 1 st, turn, p5, turn, sl 2nd, 3rd, 4th, and 5th sts over 1st st, k tbl of st.

Stitch 131
Four-spot lace stitch
LEVEL ❶

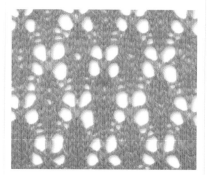

These groups of spots look like little four-petaled flowers. They show the subtle difference in the size of the holes made by working a double decrease between yarn overs and paired decreases each side of the holes.

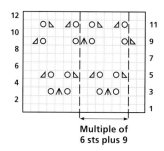

Multiple of 6 sts plus 9

Method
1st row (RS) K.
2nd and every WS row P.
3rd row K3, [yo, s2kpo, yo, k3] to end.
5th row K2, [skpo, yo, k1, yo, k2tog, k1] to last st, k1.
7th row K.
9th row K1, skpo, yo, [k3, yo, s2kpo, yo] to last 6 sts, k3, yo, k2tog, k1.
11th row K2, yo, k2tog, [k1, skpo, yo, k1, yo, k2tog] to last 5 sts, k1, skpo, yo, k2.
12th row P.
These 12 rows form the pattern.

Stitch 132
Confetti
LEVEL ❶

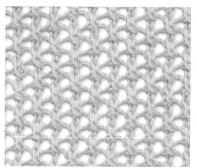

This old-fashioned allover pattern is easy to work and yet produces an interesting mixture of open mesh and a raised texture.

Multiple of 4 sts plus 2

Method
1st row (RS) K1, [yo, k1, yo, sk2po] to last st, k1.
2nd row P.
3rd row K1, [sk2po, yo, k1, yo] to last st, k1.
4th row P.
These 4 rows form the pattern.

k on RS, p on WS   ⟋ k2tog   ⟍ skpo   ⋀ s2kpo   ⟋ sk2po   O yo

Stitch 133
Harebell
LEVEL ①

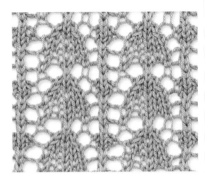

The effect of small bell-like flowers outlined with lace is enhanced by a specific type of double decrease, which gives a smooth appearance to the stitch.

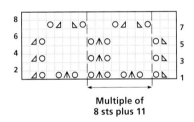

Multiple of
8 sts plus 11

Method

1st row (RS) K1, skpo, yo, [k1, yo, s2kpo, yo] to last 4 sts, k1, yo, k2tog, k1.

2nd and WS rows P.

3rd row K1, skpo, yo, [k5, yo, s2kpo, yo] to last 8 sts, k5, yo, k2tog, k1.

5th row As 3rd row.

7th row K3, [yo, skpo, k1, k2tog, yo, k3] to end.

8th row P.

These 8 rows form the pattern.

Stitch 134
Little rose lace stitch
LEVEL ①

This spot design is made with groups of yarn overs and decreases arranged to make little flower shapes in the style of a Shetland lace pattern.

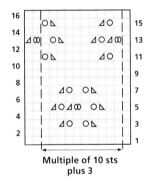

Multiple of 10 sts
plus 3

Specific symbol

⦿ Yo twice, dropping one strand on following row.

Method

1st row (RS) K.

2nd, 4th, 8th, 10th, and 12th rows P.

3rd row K4, [skpo, yo, k1, yo, k2tog, k5] to last 9 sts, skpo, yo, k1, yo, k2tog, k4.

5th row K3, [skpo, yo, k1, yo twice, k2tog, yo, k2tog, k3] to end.

6th row P, dropping one strand of each double yo.

7th row As 3rd row.

9th row K.

11th row K2, yo, k2tog, [k5, skpo, yo, k1, yo, k2tog] to last 9 sts, k5, skpo, yo, k2.

13th row K1, yo twice, k2tog, yo, k2tog, [k3, skpo, yo, k1, yo twice, k2tog, yo, k2tog] to last 8 sts, k3, skpo, yo, k1, yo twice, k2tog.

14th row As 6th row.

15th row As 11th row.

16th row P.

These 16 rows form the pattern.

Stitch 135

Little fan stitch

LEVEL 2

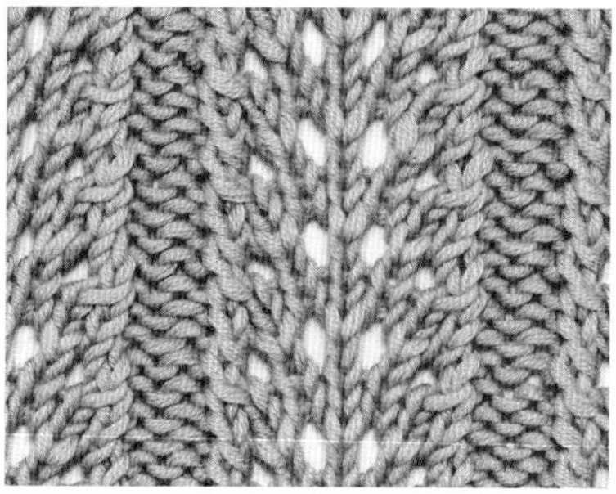

Here the yarn-over increases and the decreases are arranged in panels. Two of the four increases that make the curved rows of holes are not compensated for on the same row, but are delayed until the next right-side row, so the stitch count varies.

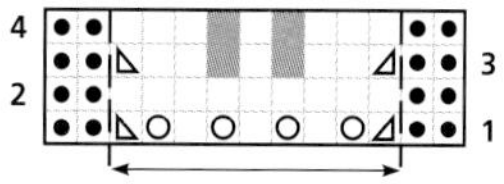

Multiple of 9 sts plus 2, with a variable stitch count

Method

1st row (RS) * P2, k2tog, [yo, k1] 3 times, yo, skpo, rep from * to last 2 sts, p2.

2nd row [K2, p9] to last 2 sts, k2.

3rd row [P2, k2tog, k5, skpo] to last 2 sts, p2.

4th row [K2, p7] to last 2 sts, k2.

These 4 rows form the pattern.

Stitch 136

Zigzag lace

LEVEL 2

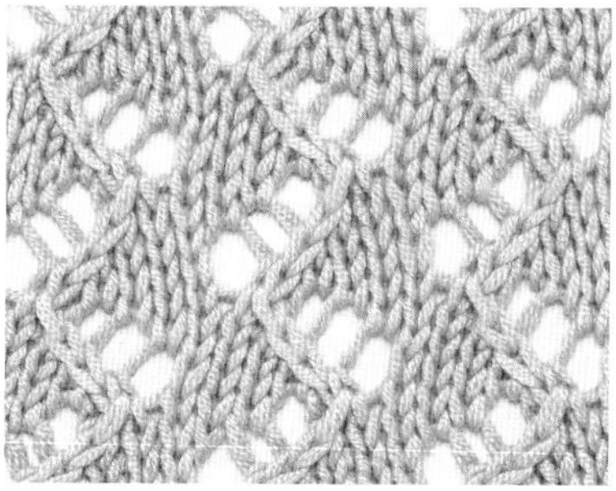

Columns of decreases and yarn overs make a pattern of zigzags in a stockinette stitch background. Once you can decrease on wrong-side rows, this is an easy pattern to work.

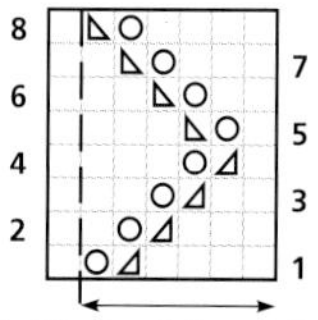

Multiple of 6 sts plus 1

Specific symbols

K2tog on RS rows, p2tog on WS rows.

Skpo on RS rows, ssp on WS rows.

Method

1st row (RS) [K4, k2tog, yo] to last st, k1.

2nd row P2, [yo, p2tog, p4] to last 5 sts, yo, p2tog, p3.

3rd row K2, [k2tog, yo, k4] to last 5 sts, k2tog, yo, k3.

4th row [P4, yo, p2tog] to last st, p1.

5th row K1, [yo, skpo, k4] to end.

6th row P3, [ssp, yo, p4] to last 4 sts, ssp, yo, p2.

7th row K3, [yo, skpo, k4] to last 4 sts, yo, skpo, k2.

8th row P1, [ssp, yo, p4] to end.

These 8 rows form the pattern.

Stitch 137

Chevron lace

LEVEL 2

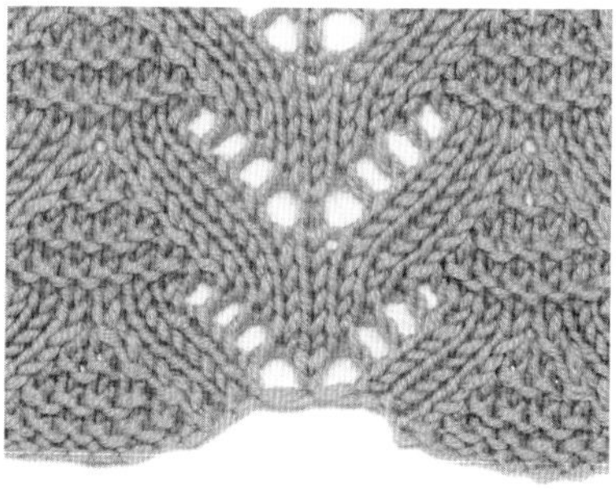

Although this lace pattern, with its graceful curving lines, looks complicated, it's very easy to do because the stitch count is constant and every wrong-side row is just purl.

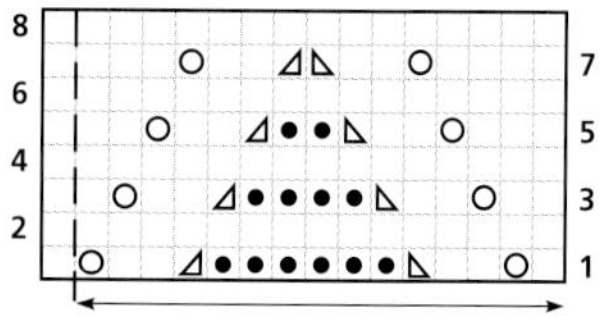

Multiple of 15 sts plus 1

Method

1st row (RS) [K1, yo, k2, skpo, p6, k2tog, k2, yo] to last st, k1.

2nd and every WS row P.

3rd row [K2, yo, k2, skpo, p4, k2tog, k2, yo, k1] to last st, k1.

5th row [K3, yo, k2, skpo, p2, k2tog, k2, yo, k2] to last st, k1.

7th row [K4, yo, k2, skpo, k2tog, k2, yo, k3] to last st, k1.

8th row P.

These 8 rows form the pattern.

88–89 Basic symbols

k on RS, p on WS · p on RS, k on WS · k tbl on RS · k2tog · skpo · s2kpo · sk2po · yo · no st

Stitch 138
Daisy and ladder
LEVEL ❷

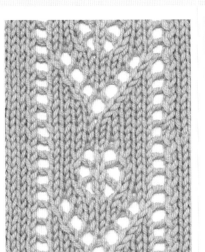

In this panel, the positioning of single yarn overs and related decreases produces an appearance of flower heads, leaves, and outlining ladders.

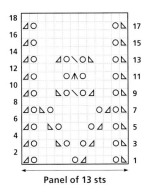

Panel of 13 sts

Stitch 139
Crocus stitch
LEVEL ❷

Groups of diagonals draw the stylized leaves and flowers that form this simple lace panel.

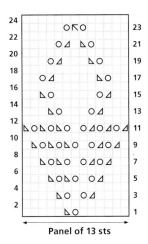

Panel of 13 sts

Stitch 140
Jeweled heart
LEVEL ❷

This simple heart, set on a reverse-stockinette-stitch background, is decorated with an internal diamond motif.

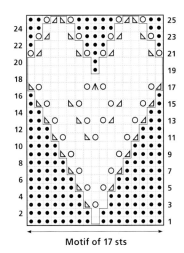

Motif of 17 sts

Stitch 141
Bird's eye LEVEL ❷

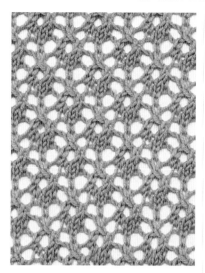

This would be a small leaf pattern if it weren't for the central eyelet in each repeat that gives this stitch its name.

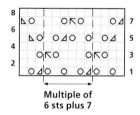

Multiple of 6 sts plus 7

Stitch 142
Lacy paisley LEVEL ❷

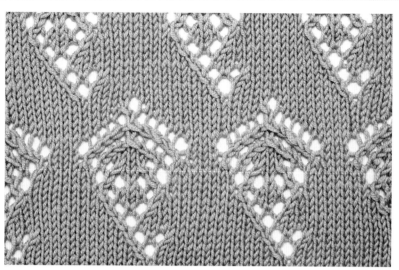

This paisley-style half-drop pattern is one of many variations on the Shetland fern stitch. The paisleys could be isolated and used as motifs, or rows one to twenty-one could be used as a border.

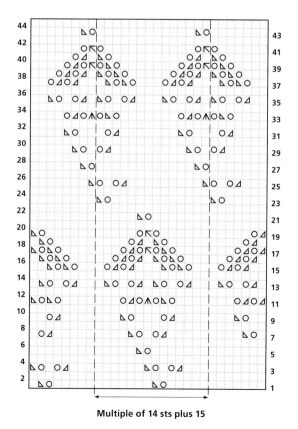

Multiple of 14 sts plus 15

☐ k on RS, p on WS   ● p on RS, k on WS   ◢ k2tog on RS, p2tog on WS   ◣ skpo on RS, p2tog tbl on WS   ⋀ s2kpo   ◥ sk2po

Stitch 143
Trellis and vine LEVEL ❷

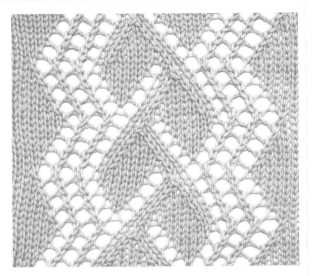

Stitch 144
Moon flower LEVEL ❷

With its bold diagonals, this old design suggests leaves and stems against an airy trellis. Here it's used as a panel, although it could be repeated for a more elaborate effect.

This imaginary flower is crisply drawn, with single ribs suggesting veins on the leaves.

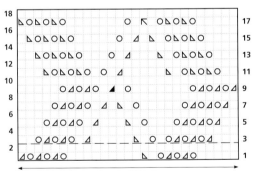

Panel of 27 sts

Specific symbol
◢ Skpo, sl st just made to L needle, sl next st over it, sl st back to R needle.

Note
Rows 3–18 form the pattern.

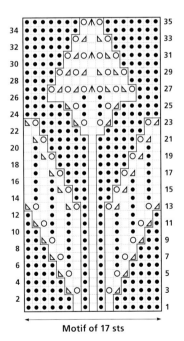

Motif of 17 sts

Stitch 145
Crisscross
LEVEL ❷

The directional quality of the parallel decreases defines this X-shaped motif. It could be used to complement textured stitches or other lace stitches.

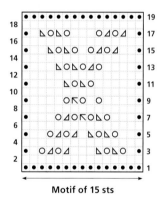

Motif of 15 sts

Stitch 146
Filigree heart
LEVEL ❷

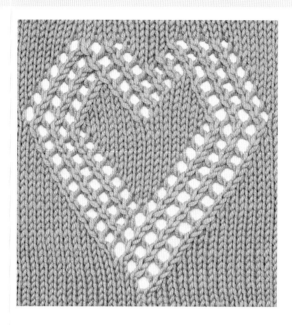

You can work just one pretty heart motif on the front of a sweater or repeat it, perhaps outlined with ribs or faggot stitch to make a panel.

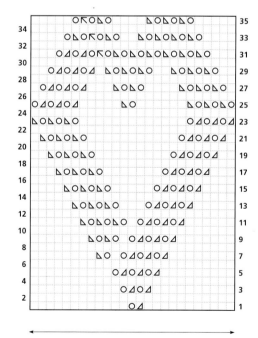

Motif of 25 sts

k on RS, p on WS p on RS, k on WS k2tog skpo s2kpo sk2po yo

Stitch 147

Diamond within a diamond

LEVEL ❷

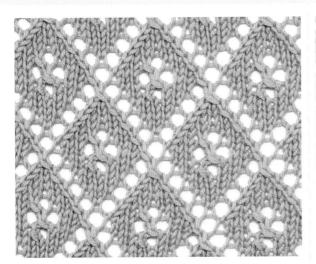

This lace has easy-to-follow progressions, which produce a design that looks more complex than it actually is.

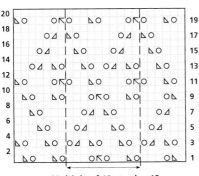

Multiple of 10 sts plus 13

Stitch 148

Double-diamond mesh

LEVEL ❷

This busy pattern with its diamonds within diamonds, set closely together, looks complicated but is actually easy to work because every wrong-side row is just purl.

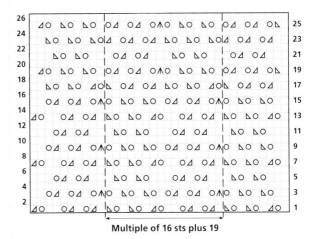

Multiple of 16 sts plus 19

Stitch 149
Drooping dayflower LEVEL ❷

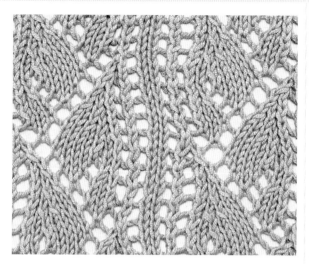

This pretty stitch can be repeated as shown to make an allover lace pattern, or you can choose to work just the center fifteen stitches as a panel. The design is based on an antique stitch pattern that has a very variable stitch count. This extended version is easy to knit because the stitch count is the same on every row.

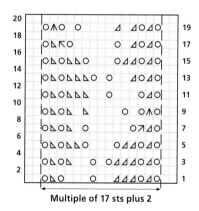

Multiple of 17 sts plus 2

Stitch 150
Triangles LEVEL ❷

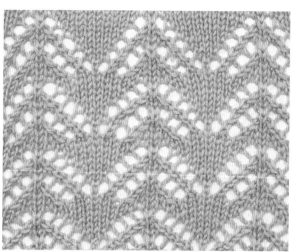

Triangles of openwork alternate with triangles of stockinette stitch in this simple but effective lace pattern. Work just rows one to ten for a pretty border pattern.

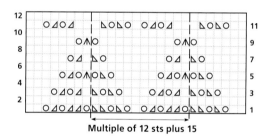

Multiple of 12 sts plus 15

Note

Rows 3–12 form the pattern.

☐ k on RS, p on WS k2tog skpo s2kpo k3tog sk2po O yo ✕╲ c2b

Stitch 151
Two-spot trellis LEVEL ❷

This sophisticated lace trellis pattern uses a three-stitch cable to carry the lines made by the paired decreases neatly to the next line of diamonds. You could omit the pairs of holes at the center of each diamond—just ignore the yarn-over and double-decrease symbols and knit the three stitches instead.

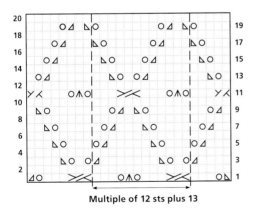

Multiple of 12 sts plus 13

Specific symbol
Sl2 to cable needle, hold at back, k1, sl nearest st from cable needle to L needle and hold cable needle at front, k1, k rem st from cable needle.

Note
A cable needle is required.

Stitch 152
Outlined diamonds LEVEL ❷

The subtle, engraved-surface effect of this stitch pattern is created by working the paired decreases one stitch away from the corresponding yarn-over increases. You could add to the texture by filling the diamonds with a simple knit and purl stitch pattern instead of stockinette stitch.

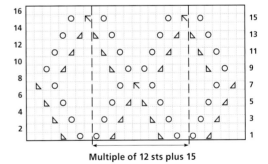

Multiple of 12 sts plus 15

Stitch 153
Tulip LEVEL ❷

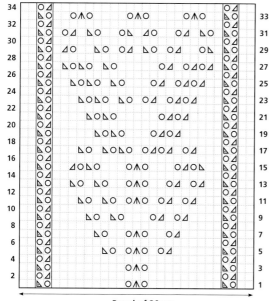

Here decreases and yarn overs form an openwork, stylized tulip. You could use the two-stitch faggot pattern that edges the panel to lighten a solid fabric.

Panel of 29 sts

Specific symbols

◿ K2tog on RS, p2tog on WS
◺ P2tog on RS

Stitch 154
Little branches LEVEL ❷

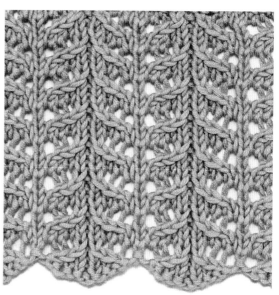

Although there are just a few rows in this pattern, it looks complex because there is decreasing and working yarn overs on both wrong-side and right-side rows.

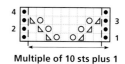

Multiple of 10 sts plus 1

Specific symbols

◿ K2tog on RS rows, p2tog on WS rows.
◺ Skpo on RS rows, ssp on WS rows.

Method

1st row (RS) [P1, k2, k2tog, yo, k1, yo, skpo, k2] to last st, p1.
2nd row [K1, p1, ssp, yo, p3, yo, p2tog, p1] to last st, k1.
3rd row [P1, k2tog, yo, k5, yo, skpo] to last st, p1.
4th row [K1, p9] to last st, k1.
These 4 rows form the pattern.

☐ k on RS, p on WS   ● p on RS, k on WS   ◿ k2tog   ◺ skpo   ⋀ s2kpo   O yo

Stitch 155
Lily LEVEL ❷

The use of three different decreases shapes this simple flower on a smooth stockinette-stitch background.

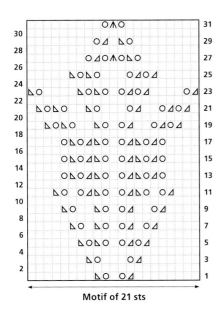

Motif of 21 sts

Stitch 156
Cockleshells LEVEL ❸

This pretty pattern creates an openwork effect with a row of extra-long stitches made by wrapping the yarn around the needle three times for each stitch. It isn't identical on both sides, but the wrong side looks lovely too, making it ideal for scarves and wraps.

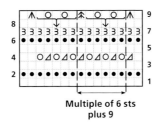

Multiple of 6 sts plus 9

Specific symbols

⊿ P2tog on WS.

3 K, wrapping yarn around needle 3 times for each st, dropping extra wraps on next row to make a long st.

Work bracketed sts in st indicated in row below.

🔾 S3k2po: Sl3 knitwise, k2tog, pass slipped sts over.

Method

1st row (RS) K.

2nd row K.

3rd row K.

4th row P2, [yo, p2tog] to last st, p1.

5th row K.

6th row K.

7th row K, wrapping yarn around needle 3 times for each st.

8th row P, dropping the extra wraps to make long stitches.

9th row K1, s2kpo, * (k1, yo, k1, yo, k1) all in next st in row below, s3k2po, rep from * to last 5 sts, (k1, yo, k1, yo, k1) all in next st in row below, s2kpo, k1.

Rows 2–9 form the pattern.

Stitch 157
Ribbed leaves LEVEL ❸

This pattern of a leaf within a diamond is unusual in that it uses rib to texture the leaves. The rib appears like veins.

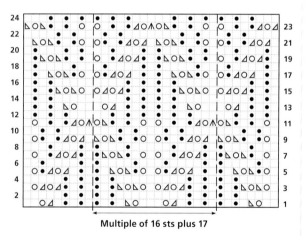

Multiple of 16 sts plus 17

Stitch 158
Flower garden LEVEL ❸

A combination of patterns on every row gives this design its graceful curves. It also contrasts stockinette stitch and reverse stockinette stitch.

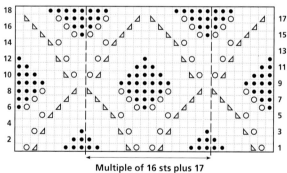

Multiple of 16 sts plus 17

Specific symbols

◩ K2tog on RS, p2tog on WS.
◪ Skpo on RS, p2tog tbl on WS.

☐ k on RS, p on WS ● p on RS, k on WS ◪ k2tog ◣ skpo ▲ s2kpo ◥ sk2po ○ yo

Stitch 159
Fern lace LEVEL ❸

This pattern is based on a Shetland lace stitch but with the decreases paired to give a cleaner line to the motifs. Watch out for the yarn overs and decreases on wrong-side rows at the top of each band of motifs.

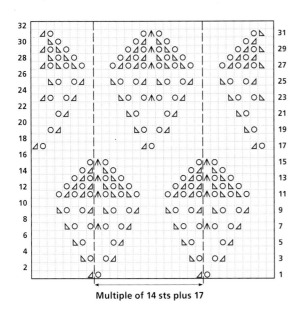

Multiple of 14 sts plus 17

Specific symbols
⊿ K2tog on RS, p2tog on WS.
◣ Skpo on RS, ssp on WS.

Stitch 160
Falling leaves LEVEL ❸

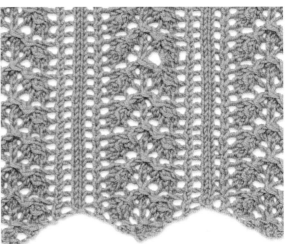

This old-fashioned stitch has the appearance of pairs of leaves between ladders. It also creates a decorative scalloped edge at both cast-on and cast-off edges.

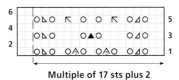

Multiple of 17 sts plus 2

Specific symbols
⬚ Sl1, k3tog, psso.
▲ Sl1, k4tog, psso.

Stitch 161
Leaf and bud lace   LEVEL ❸

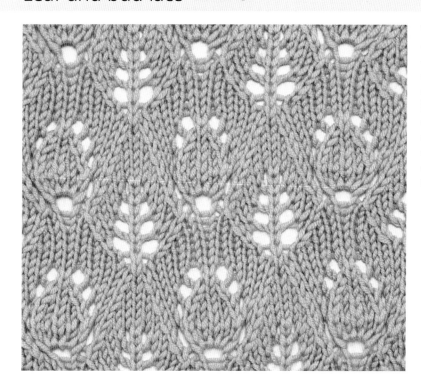

This fancy lace-stitch pattern has a little of everything—yarn overs and paired decreases on right-side rows, plus a varying stitch count shown in the chart for the bud between the leaves. But despite all these tricks, it's not difficult to work, as once you've completed the first repeat, it's easy to see where you are in the pattern.

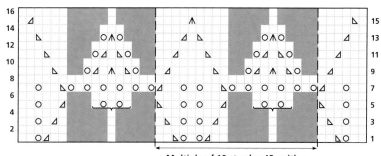

Multiple of 10 sts plus 13, with a variable stitch count

Specific symbol

 (K1, yo, k1, yo, k1) all in st indicated by bracket.

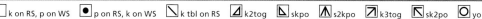 k on RS, p on WS   ● p on RS, k on WS   ◣ k tbl on RS   ◿ k2tog   ◣ skpo   ⋀ s2kpo   ⬈ k3tog   ◥ sk2po   ◯ yo

Stitch 162
Daisy lace LEVEL ❸

The lower leaves of these daisies arch rather elegantly over the flowers below, although the patterning is all on right-side rows.

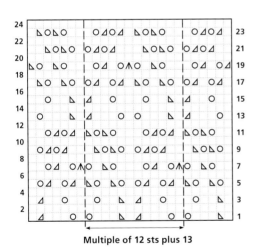

Multiple of 12 sts plus 13

Stitch 163
Floret LEVEL ❸

The centers of these lacy flowers form tiny leaves, making a subtle design within a design.

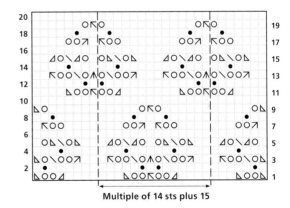

Multiple of 14 sts plus 15

Notes

• On WS rows, the double yarn over is worked (p1, k1) before the center of each motif and (k1, p1) after the center.

• There are three types of double decreases.

▨ no st

Stitch 164
Butterfly motif LEVEL ❸

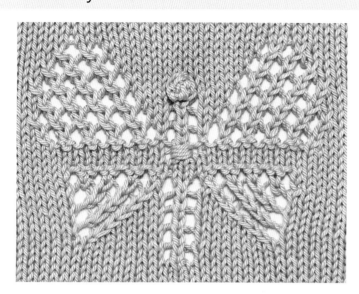

Lacy stitches and fine yarn suggest the fragility of a butterfly and yet outline the insect's structure very clearly. The eyelet holes on the lower wings are worked on every row, but those on the upper wings are worked on right-side rows only.

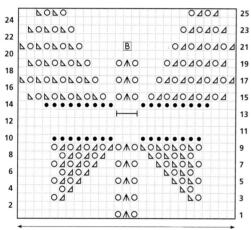

Motif of 27 sts

Specific symbols

B (K1, p1, k1, p1, k1) all in 1 st, turn, p5, turn, sl 2nd, 3rd, 4th, and 5th sts over 1st st, k tbl.

⊢—⊣ K3, sl them to cable needle, take yarn around them counterclockwise (from above) 4 times ending WS, sl sts back to R needle.

◿ K2tog on RS, p2tog on WS.

◸ Skpo on RS, p2tog tbl on WS.

Note

A cable needle is required.

Stitch 165
Small butterfly motif LEVEL ❸

This is a development of an old stitch sometimes called honeybee, with two large eyelets forming the lower wings.

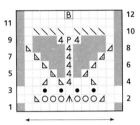

Motif of 11 sts, with a
variable stitch count

Specific symbols

⌷4⌷ Yo 4 times; on rows 5–8, follow by dropping yos of previous row.

◥ K in back of yo.

⌷P⌷ Dropping yos of previous row, lift 5 long strands to L needle and p1, enclosing all strands.

⌷B⌷ (K1, p1, k1) all in 1 st, turn, p3, turn, sl 2nd and 3rd sts over 1st st, k tbl.

◿ P2tog on WS.

◣ P2tog tbl on WS.

Note

This design begins on a WS row.

Stitch 166
Seaweed stitch LEVEL ❸

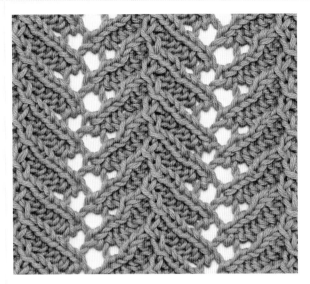

Converging ribs give this lacy stitch the appearance of soft fronds. It needn't be an allover pattern since a few four-row repeats make a very pretty edging (see *Using the stitches*, page 186).

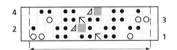

Multiple of 14 sts plus 2,
with a variable stitch count

Specific symbols

◥ Wyab, sk2po.

◿ P2tog on WS.

◿ K2tog on WS.

Note

The stitch count increases on the very first row and then alternates between rows.

STITCH SELECTOR Bobbles and Leaves

Bobbles and leaves always create an impact, because their three-dimensional look really mimics natural objects. Don't be intimidated by the instructions. Once you understand working into a multiple increase, they're not too difficult and the result will be very special.

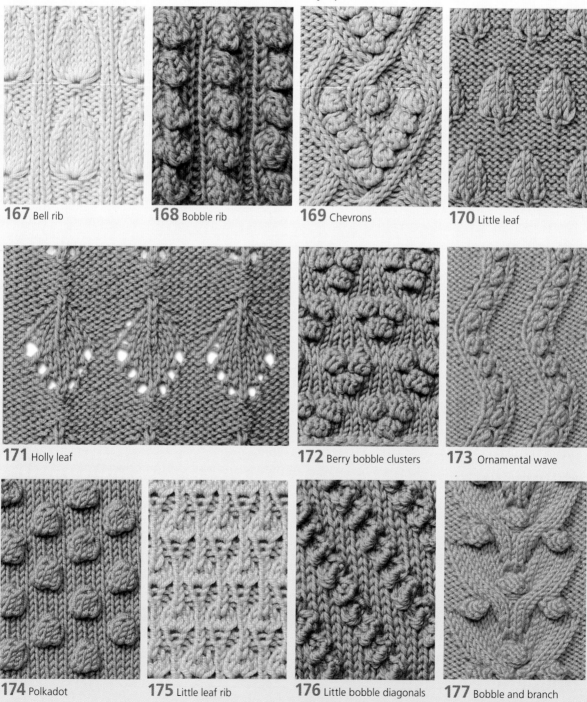

167 Bell rib

168 Bobble rib

169 Chevrons

170 Little leaf

171 Holly leaf

172 Berry bobble clusters

173 Ornamental wave

174 Polkadot

175 Little leaf rib

176 Little bobble diagonals

177 Bobble and branch

178 Bobble diamond net

179 Cockade

180 Twin leaves

181 Arrowhead

182 Diamond knots

183 Jack-in-the-box

184 Formal leaf

185 Sunflower

186 Leaf and swag

187 Sprig

188 Trailing branch

BOBBLES AND LEAVES—CONTINUED

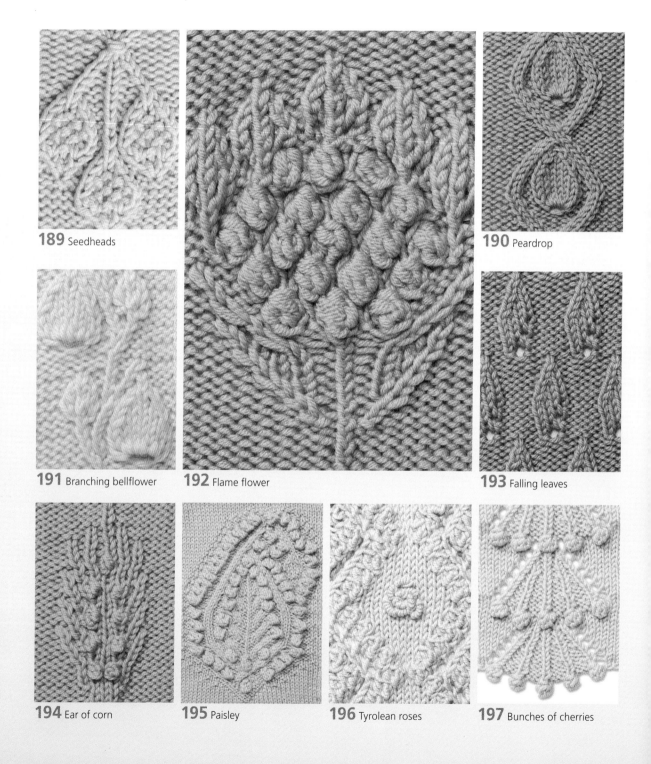

189 Seedheads

190 Peardrop

191 Branching bellflower

192 Flame flower

193 Falling leaves

194 Ear of corn

195 Paisley

196 Tyrolean roses

197 Bunches of cherries

198 Leafy vine

199 Lime leaf

200 Flame leaves

201 Embellished cable

202 Plume

203 Leaf within a diamond

204 Bunch of grapes

205 Leaves and berries

Stitch 167
Bell rib
LEVEL 1

Panels of bells and two-stitch ribs are alternated here. For a single panel of bells, work the center five stitches from the chart or add more rib between the bells.

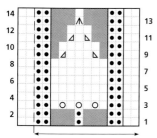

7 sts plus 2, with a variable st count

Method
1st row (RS) K2, [p5, k2] to end.

2nd row P2, [k5, p2] to end.

3rd row K2, * p2, [k1, yo, k1, yo, k1, yo, k1] all in next st, p2, k2, rep from * to end.

4th row P2, [k2, p7, k2, p2] to end.

5th row K2, [p2, k7, p2, k2] to end.

6th, 7th, and 8th rows As 4th, 5th, and 4th rows.

9th row K2, [p2, skpo, k3, k2tog, p2, k2] to end.

10th row P2, [k2, p5, k2, p2] to end.

11th row K2, [p2, skpo, k1, k2tog, p2, k2] to end.

12th row P2, [k2, p3, k2, p2] to end.

13th row K2, [p2, s2kpo, p2, k2] to end.

14th row P2, [k2, p1, k2, p2] to end.

These 14 rows form the pattern.

Stitch 168
Bobble rib
LEVEL 1

This very simple pattern places rows of bobbles on the center stitch of a three-stitch and two-stitch rib. For a less dense effect, space the bobbles farther apart or work more plain rib between ribs with bobbles.

Multiple of 5 sts plus 2

Specific symbol
B **Mb**: (K1, yo, k1, yo, k1) all in 1 st, turn, p5, turn, k5, turn, p5, turn, sl3 sts as if to k3tog, k2tog, pass slipped sts over.

Method
1st row (RS) P2, [k3, p2] to end.

2nd row K2, [p3, k2] to end.

3rd row P2, [k1, mb, k1, p2] to end.

4th row As 2nd row.

These 4 rows form the pattern.

Stitch 169
Chevrons
LEVEL 1

Bobbles can be used to complement cables in many different ways. Here nine bobbles emphasize a chevron and one studs the center of the formation.

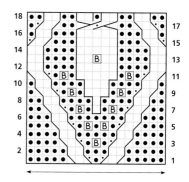

Panel of 17 sts

Specific symbols
B (K1, p1, k1, p1, k1) all in 1 st, turn, p5, turn, pass 4 sts just made, 1 at a time, over end st, k tbl.

Sl3 to cable needle, hold at back, k2, sl nearest st from cable needle back to L needle, p, k rem 2 sts from cable needle.

Note
A cable needle is required.

k on RS, p on WS p on RS, k on WS k tbl on RS, p tbl on WS k2tog skpo s2kpo O yo no st

Stitch 170
Little leaf
LEVEL ①

This versatile pattern has alternating rows of embossed leaves on a reverse-stockinette-stitch background. The leaf motifs alternate, but if you want them to line up, repeat rows one to twelve.

Method

1st row (RS) P.
2nd row K.
3rd row P3, [k1 tbl, p5] to last 4 sts, k1 tbl, p3.
4th row K3, p1 tbl, [k5, p1 tbl] to last 3 sts, k3.
5th row P3, * (m1R, yo, k1 tbl, yo, m1L) all in next st, p5, rep from * to last 4 sts, (m1R, yo, k1 tbl, yo, m1L) all in next st, p3.
6th row K3, p5, [k5, p5] to last 3 sts, k3.
7th row P3, [k5, p5] to last 8 sts, k5, p3.
8th row As 6th row.
9th row P3, [skpo, k1, k2tog, p5] to last 8 sts, skpo, k1, k2tog, p3.
10th row K3, p3, [k5, p3] to last 3 sts, k3.
11th row P3, [s2kpo, p5] to last 6 sts, s2kpo, p3.
12th row K.
13th row P.
14th row K.
15th row P6, [k1 tbl, p5] to last st, p1.
16th row K6, [p1 tbl, k5] to last st, k1.
17th row P6, * (m1R, yo, k1 tbl, yo, m1L) all in next st, p5, rep from * to last st, p1.
18th row K6, [p5, k5] to last st, k1.
19th row P6, [k5, p5] to last st, p1.
20th row As 18th row.
21st row P6, [skpo, k1, k2tog, p5] to last st, p1.
22nd row K6, [p3, k5] to last st, k1.
23rd row P6, [s2kpo, p5] to last st, p1.
24th row K.
These 24 rows form the pattern.

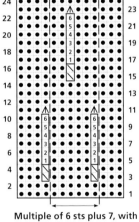

Multiple of 6 sts plus 7, with a variable st count

Leaf

Note

Work the leaf chart over one st and six rows as shown on the main chart.

◤◢ c3bp   ◥◣ c3fp   ⋒ m1L   ⋒ m1R

Stitch 171
Holly leaf
LEVEL ❶

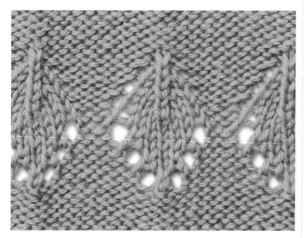

The stitch count remains the same throughout this design, and so the leaves, although well defined, are not raised on the surface of the fabric.

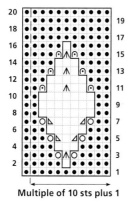

Multiple of 10 sts plus 1

Stitch 172
Berry bobble clusters
LEVEL ❶

If you love the way bobbles look, but hate turning the work, this is the pattern for you. Each of these nubbly bobbles is worked over two rows, increasing to create the base of each bobble on right-side rows and decreasing each bobble back to one stitch on wrong-side rows.

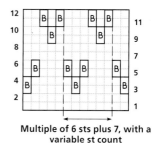

Multiple of 6 sts plus 7, with a variable st count

Specific symbol

B **1st row** (RS) (K1, yo, k1, yo, k1) all in 1 st.
2nd row (WS) K5, pass 4 sts just made, 1 at a time, over end st.

☐ k on RS, p on WS ● p on RS, k on WS ╲ k tbl on RS p tbl on WS   k2tog   skpo   s2kpo m1p   yo

Stitch 173
Ornamental wave
LEVEL ❶

Increases and decreases, not cables, are used to make these gentle curves. They are decorated with small, neat bobbles.

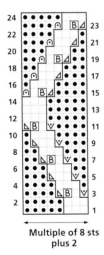

Multiple of 8 sts
plus 2

Specific symbols
B (K1, p1, k1) all in 1 st, turn, p3, turn, pass 2 of sts just made, 1 at a time, over end st, k tbl.

◻ K1 tbl on WS.

Stitch 174
Polkadot
LEVEL ❶

These bold bobbles are well defined in spite of being in stockinette stitch on a stockinette-stitch ground. Their size and spacing can, of course, be adapted to fit in with other stitch patterns.

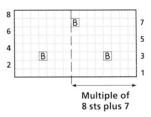

Multiple of
8 sts plus 7

Specific symbol
B **Mb:** (K tfl, tbl, tfl, tbl, and tfl) of 1 st, turn, p5, turn, k5, turn, p5, turn, pass 4 of sts just made, 1 at a time, over end st, k tbl.

Method
1st row (RS) K.
2nd and WS rows P.
3rd row K3, [mb, k7] to last 4 sts, mb, k3.
5th row K.
7th row [K7, mb] to last 7 sts, k7.
8th row P.
These 8 rows form the pattern.

Stitch 175

Little leaf rib

LEVEL 1

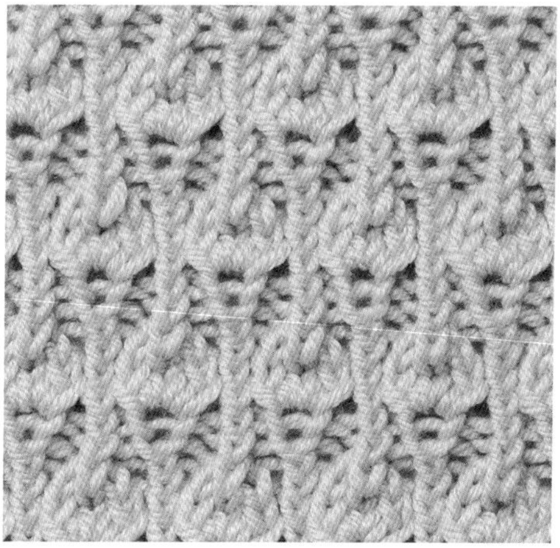

Because these leaves are formed on single rib stitches there's scope to extend the ribs below or above the stitch pattern. The leaf shapings mean that only rows six to twelve are entirely in rib.

Method

1st row (RS) * P1, (k1, yo, k1, yo, k1) all in 1 st, p1, k1; rep from * to last 3 sts, p1, (k1, yo, k1, yo, k1) all in 1 st, p1.

2nd row * K1, p5, k1, p1; rep from * to last 7 sts, k1, p5, k1.

3rd row * P1, skpo, k1, k2tog, p1, k1; rep from * to last 7 sts, p1, skpo, k1, k2tog, p1.

4th row * K1, p3, k1, p1; rep from * to last 5 sts, k1, p3, k1.

5th row * P1, s2kpo, p1, k1; rep from * to last 5 sts, p1, s2kpo, p1.

6th row K1, [p1, k1] to end.

7th row * P1, k1, p1, (k1, yo, k1, yo, k1) all in next st; rep from * to last 3 sts, p1, k1, p1.

8th row * K1, p1, k1, p5; rep from * to last 3 sts, k1, p1, k1.

9th row P1, k1, p1, skpo, k1, k2tog; rep from * to last 3 sts, p1, k1, p1.

10th row * K1, p1, k1, p3; rep from * to last 3 sts, k1, p1, k1.

11th row * P1, k1, p1, s2kpo; rep from * to last 3 sts, p1, k1, p1.

12th row As 6th row.

These 12 rows form the pattern.

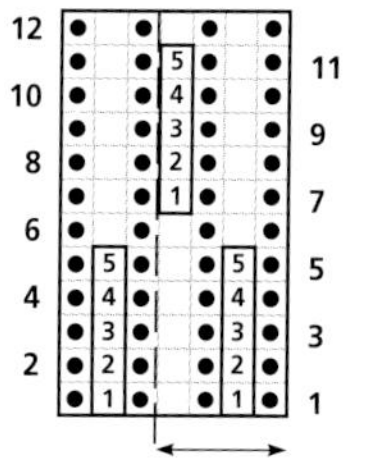

Multiple of 4 sts plus 3, with a variable st count

Leaf

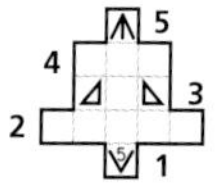

Specific symbol

(K1, yo, k1, yo, k1) all in one st.

Note

Work the leaf chart over one stitch and five rows as shown on the main chart.

Stitch 176

Little bobble diagonals

LEVEL 1

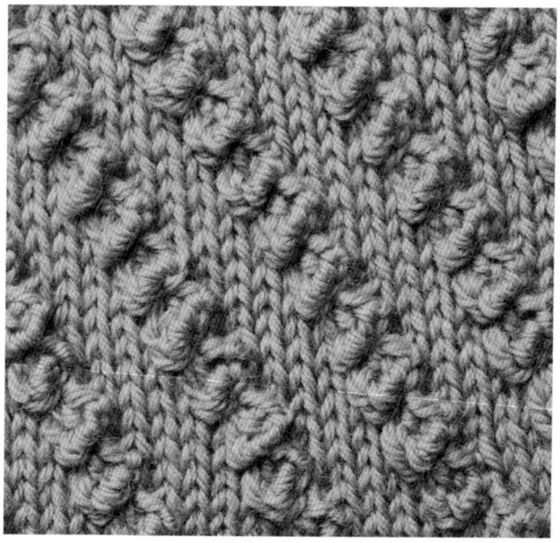

The natural tendency of these bobbles to lean to the side is emphasized by arranging them in diagonals. The stitch above each bobble is purled through the back of the loop for stability.

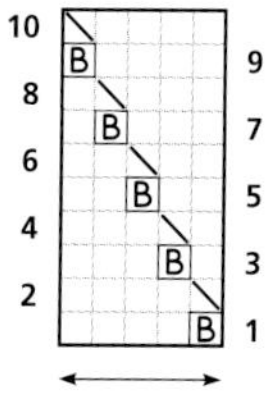

Multiple of 5 sts

Specific symbol

B **Mb**: (K1, p1, k1) all in 1 st, turn, p3, turn, k3, pass 2 of sts just made, 1 at a time, over end st.

Method

1st row (RS) [Mb, k4] to end.

2nd and WS rows P, working st above bobble tbl.

3rd row [K1, mb, k3] to end.

5th row [K2, mb, k2] to end.

7th row [K3, mb, k1] to end.

9th row [K4, mb] to end.

10th row As 2nd row.

These 10 rows form the pattern.

112–113 Basic symbols

k on RS, p on WS | p on RS, k on WS | k tbl on RS, p tbl on WS | k2tog | skpo | s2kpo | yo

Stitch 177
Bobble and branch
LEVEL ❶

Stitch 178
Bobble diamond net
LEVEL ❶

Although most of the patterning is done on one row, this nice fat cable punctuated with large bobbles is very lively.

Firm little bobbles nestle in the center of each diamond created by purl stitches on a stockinette-stitch background. If you're working this as an allover pattern on a sweater, omit the bobbles at the side edges to make a neat join at the side seams.

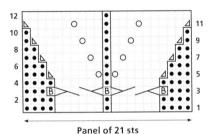

Panel of 21 sts

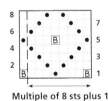

Multiple of 8 sts plus 1

Specific symbol

B (K1, yo, k1, yo, k1) all in 1 st, turn, k5, turn, p5, turn, k5, pass 4 sts just made, 1 at a time, over end st, k tbl.

Note

A cable needle is required.

Specific symbol

B **Mb**: (K1, yo, k1, yo, k1) all in 1 st, turn, k5, turn, [sl1 knitwise] 4 times, k1, pass the slipped sts over.

Method

1st row (RS) [Mb, k3, p1, k3] to last st, mb.
2nd row [P3, k1, p1, k1, p2] to last st, p1.
3rd row [K2, p1, k3, p1, k1] to last st, k1.
4th row [P1, k1, p5, k1] to last st, p1.
5th row [P1, k3, mb, k3] to last st, p1.
6th row As 4th row.
7th row As 3rd row.
8th row As 2nd row.
These 8 rows form the pattern.

c6b   c6f

Stitch 179
Cockade LEVEL ❷

Nipped in at the base and then fanning out with twist stitches and adorned with bobbles, this handsome motif could be used singly or in groups.

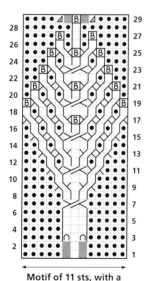

Motif of 11 sts, with a variable st count

Specific symbols

B (K1, yo, k1) all in 1 st, turn, p3, turn, k3, turn, p3, turn, s2kpo.

Sl2 to cable needle, hold at back, k1, then k2 from cable needle.

Note

A cable needle is required.

Stitch 180
Twin leaves LEVEL ❷

Although they're quite formal and symmetrical, these paired leaves derive from nature. They make a neat panel pattern.

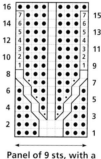

Panel of 9 sts, with a variable st count

Leaf

Specific symbol

P tbl on WS.

Notes

• Work leaf chart over one stitch and seven rows, as shown on the main chart.
• A cable needle is required.

 k on RS, p on WS   p on RS, k on WS   p2tog   k2tog   skpo   sk2po   m1   yo   m1L   m1R

Stitch 181
Arrowhead LEVEL ❷

Bobbles, cable crosses, and eyelets combine to create these incisive arrowheads, linked by a central five-stitch cable.

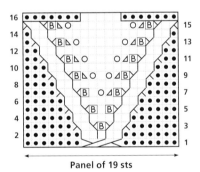

Panel of 19 sts

Specific symbols
◣◢ Sl3 to cable needle, hold at back, k2, sl nearest st from cable needle back to L needle and k this st, then k2 rem sts from cable needle.

B (K1, yo, k1) all in 1 st, turn, k3, turn, p3, pass 2 of sts just made, 1 at a time, over end st.

Note
A cable needle is required.

Stitch 182
Diamond knots LEVEL ❷

Seven-stitch knots form a rich diamond mesh. Making this knot is exactly like making a bobble, except that no turning rows are required.

Specific symbol
B Mb: (K1, yo, k1, yo, k1, yo, k1) all in 1 st, pass 2nd, 3rd, 4th, 5th, and 6th sts over 1st st.

Method
1st row [K3, mb, k2] to last st, k1.
2nd and WS rows P.
3rd row [K2, mb, k1, mb, k1] to last st, k1.
5th row [K1, mb, k3, mb] to last st, k1.
7th row [Mb, k5], mb to last st, mb.
9th row [K1, mb, k3, mb] to last st, k1.
11th row [K2, mb, k1, mb, k1] to last st, k1.
12th row P.
These 12 rows form the pattern.

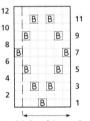

Multiple of 6 sts plus 1

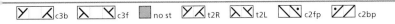

Stitch 183
Jack-in-the-box LEVEL ❷

Each diamond of the background of this cabled lattice is filled with textured stitches and a tiny bobble on a stalk. For an allover pattern, repeat the multiple of fourteen stitches, as shown.

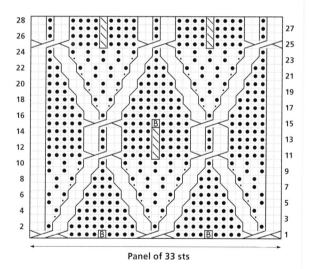

Panel of 33 sts

Specific symbols

Sl3 to cable needle, hold at back, k2, sl nearest st on cable needle to L needle, hold cable needle at front, p1, then k2 from cable needle.

B (K1, yo, k1) all in 1 st, turn, p3, turn, s2kpo.

Note

A cable needle is required.

Stitch 184
Formal leaf LEVEL ❷

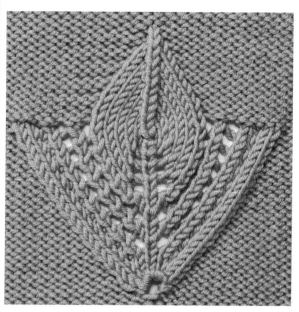

Lacy diagonals and lacy verticals both shape and decorate this single large leaf.

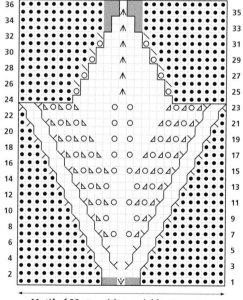

Motif of 23 sts, with a variable st count

Specific symbols

Ⓥ (K1, p1, k1, p1, k1) all in 1 st.
⊠ K tbl on WS.

Note

A cable needle is required.

 k on RS, p on WS   p on RS, k on WS   k tbl on RS, p tbl on WS   k2tog   s2kpo   skpo   yo   sk2po

Stitch 185
Sunflower LEVEL ❷

This long, narrow chart, which produces a short, round flower, illustrates what an effect stitch gauge can have on a design.

Specific symbol

B (K1, p1, k1, p1, k1) all in 1 st, turn, p5, turn, pass 4 of sts just made, 1 at a time, over end st, k tbl.

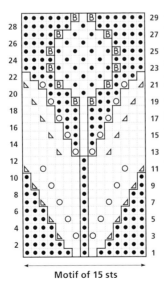

Motif of 15 sts

Stitch 186
Leaf and swag LEVEL ❷

Fit a single leaf into a chevron formation of bobbles to make a motif that can be used as an isolated motif or for a bold panel pattern, as shown here.

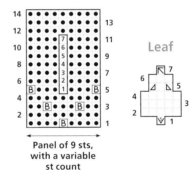

Panel of 9 sts, with a variable st count

Leaf

Specific symbols

B (K1, p1, k1, p1, k1) all in 1 st, turn, p5, turn, k5, turn, p2tog tbl, p1, p2tog, turn, sk2po.

Ⓥ (K1, p1, k1, p1, k1) all in 1 st.

Note

Work leaf chart over one stitch and seven rows, as shown on the main chart.

☐ no st   ⟋⟍ c3b   ⟋ ⟋ c3bp   ⟍ ⟍ c3f   ⟍ ⟍ c3fp

Stitch 187
Sprig LEVEL ❷

The leaf and bud on this stem are each constructed slightly differently. A final wrong-side decrease gives the bud its rounder shape, while a double decrease on the right side makes a more conventional pointed leaf.

Leaf

Bud

Motif of 5 sts, with a variable st count

Specific symbols

Ⅴ (K1, yo, k1) all in 1 st.

Ⅴ (K1, yo, k1, yo, k1) all in 1 st.

↗ Sk2po on WS.

Notes

• Work leaf chart over one stitch and six rows, as shown on the left of the main chart; work bud chart over one stitch and eleven rows, as shown on the right of the main chart.

• A cable needle is required.

Stitch 188
Trailing branch LEVEL ❷

Twisted ribs emphasize the curves of these cabled branches, which end in tight clusters of bobbles.

Specific symbols

B (K1, yo, k1, yo, k1) all in 1 st, turn, k5, turn, p5, pass 4 of sts just made, 1 at a time, over end st.

⟍⟍⟍ Sl3 to cable needle, hold at front, p1, then k1 tbl, p1, k1 tbl from cable needle.

⟋⟋⟋ Sl1 to cable needle, hold at back, k1 tbl, p1, k1 tbl, then p1 from cable needle.

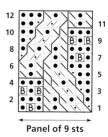

Panel of 9 sts

Note

A cable needle is required.

 k on RS, p on WS   p on RS, k on WS k tbl on RS, p tbl on WS   k2tog skpo s2kpo sk2po   c2f

Stitch 189
Seedheads   LEVEL ❷

To create the illusion that these seedheads are tied together is very simple. It's done by winding the yarn around several stitches to close them up; a technique that can be used to create a smocked effect.

Stitch 190
Peardrop   LEVEL ❷

Large bells, apparently suspended in a diamond cable, fill out the design in a very satisfying way.

Specific symbols

⊢——⊣ K3, sl these 3 sts to cable needle, take yarn around them (counterclockwise from above) 4 times, ending WS, sl sts back to R needle.

Ⅴ (K1 tbl, k1) all in 1 st, then insert left needle behind vertical strand running down between sts just made and k this strand tbl.

Seedhead

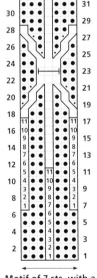

Motif of 7 sts, with a variable st count

Panel of 13 sts, with a variable st count

Bell

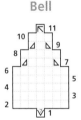

Specific symbols

▷─··─◁ Sl2 to cable needle, hold at front, sl next st to 2nd cable needle, hold at back, k2, then p1 from 2nd cable needle, then k2 from 1st cable needle.

Ⅴ (K1, yo, k1, yo, k1, yo, k1) all in one st.

Notes

- Starting on the seventh row, work bell chart over one stitch and eleven rows, as shown on the main chart.
- Two cable needles are required.

Notes

- Work the seedhead chart over one stitch and eleven rows, as shown on the main chart.
- A cable needle is required.

 c2f   c2bp    c3bp   c3fp   m1

Stitch 191
Branching bellflower LEVEL ②

This pretty little panel alternates simple bell-shaped flowers with tiny leaves on a twisted-stitch stem. If you want to knit a single motif, work rows one to fourteen, omitting the double wrap on row fourteen and working reverse stockinette stitch instead of the center stem stitches from row nine onward.

Notes

- Work the flower chart over one stitch and nine rows, as shown on the lower right and top left of the main chart. Work the leaf chart over one stitch and five rows, as shown on the lower left and top right of the main chart.
- Rows two to twenty-five form the pattern.
- A cable needle is required.

Specific symbols

SI1 to cable needle, hold at back, k1 tbl, then k1 tbl from cable needle.

SI1 to cable needle, hold at front, p1, then k1 tbl from cable needle.

SI1 to cable needle, hold at front, k1 tbl, then k1 tbl from cable needle.

SI1 to cable needle, hold at back, k1 tbl, then p1 from cable needle.

Yo twice when purling this st; drop 2nd yo on next row.

Leaf

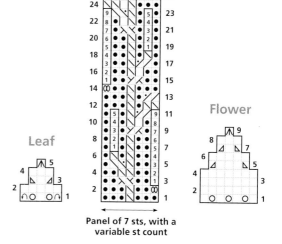

Flower

Panel of 7 sts, with a variable st count

 k on RS, p on WS   p on RS, k on WS   k tbl on RS, p tb1 on WS   k2tog   skpo   s2kpo   yo   c2b

Stitch 192
Flame flower LEVEL ②

Although this richly textured motif looks complex, it's quite easy to do. On every wrong-side row you just knit and purl the stitches as shown.

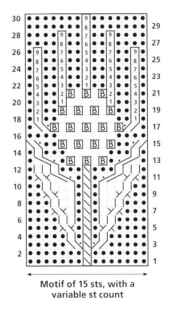

Motif of 15 sts, with a variable st count

Petal

Specific symbols

Sl2 to cable needle, hold at back, k1, then p2 from cable needle.

Sl1 to cable needle, hold at front, p2, then k1 from cable needle.

B (K1, yo, k1, yo, k1) all in 1 st, turn, p5, turn, [sl1 knitwise] 4 times, k1, pass slipped sts over.

Notes

• Work petals over one stitch and nine rows, as indicated on the main chart.
• A cable needle is required.

⟍⟍ c2fp   ⟍⟋ c2f   ⟋⟋ c2bp   ⌒ m1R   ⌒ m1L

Stitch 193
Falling leaves LEVEL ❷

The leaves in this half-drop repeat are very easy to knit, since they have only one type of increase and one type of decrease. This gives them their furled appearance.

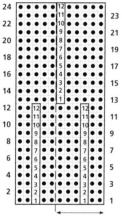

Multiple of 6 sts plus 5, with a variable st count

Note

Work leaf chart over one stitch and twelve rows, as shown on the main chart.

Leaf

Stitch 194
Ear of corn LEVEL ❷

Natural objects and knitting are curiously compatible. For example, small tight knots and single cable stitches make a perfect stylized ear of corn.

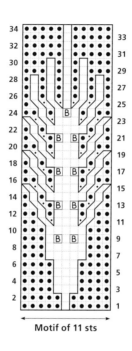

Motif of 11 sts

Specific symbol

B (K1, p1, k1, p1, k1) all in 1 st, pass 4 of sts just made, 1 at a time, over end st.

Note

A cable needle is required.

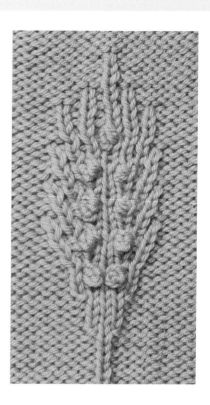

☐ k on RS, p on WS   ● p on RS, k on WS   ◗ k tbl on RS, p tbl on WS   ◢ k2tog   O yo   c2fp   c2bp

Stitch 195
Paisley LEVEL ❸

This richly decorated motif looks impressive, but isn't as difficult to work as you might think. Although there are cables on some of the wrong-side rows, they are no harder to work than cables on a right-side row. The remaining wrong-side rows are knit and purl.

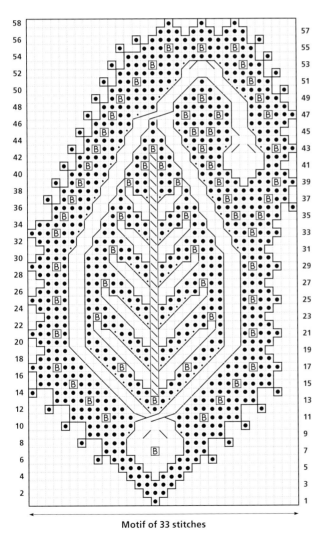

Motif of 33 stitches

Specific symbols

B̲ (K1, p1, k1, p1, k1) all in 1 st, turn, p5, turn, k2tog, k1, skpo, turn, p3, turn, s2kpo.

◥◣ On RS, sl2 to cable needle, hold at front, p1, then k2 from cable needle; on WS, sl next st to cable needle, hold at front, p2, then k1 from cable needle.

◹◿ On RS rows, sl next st to cable needle, hold at back, k2, then p1 from cable needle; on WS rows, sl2 to cable needle, hold at back, k1, then p2 from cable needle.

◤◥◣◢ Sl3 to cable needle, hold at back, k2, sl nearest st on cable needle to L needle, hold cable needle at front, p1, then k2 from cable needle.

◿◿ Sl3 to cable needle, hold at back, k2, then p3 from cable needle.

Note

A cable needle is required.

Stitch 196
Tyrolean roses LEVEL ❸

Combining embroidery with raised stitch patterns was a feature of 1930s' Austrian-style knitting. In this update, bullion-knot roses have been added to bobbled diamonds.

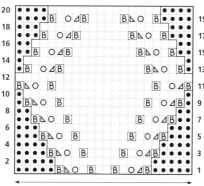

Panel of 22 sts

Specific symbol

B (K1, p1, k1) all in 1 st, turn, p3, turn, k3, pass 2 of sts just made, 1 at a time, over end st.

Note

The bullion knots are not denoted in the chart, but are simply worked in the center of the diamond.

Stitch 197
Bunches of cherries LEVEL ❸

This glorious repeat pattern starts with a bobbled edge and produces a fabric with a layered effect of ribs and bobbles.

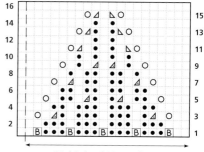

Multiple of 20 sts plus 1

Specific symbol

B (K1, p1, k1, p1, k1) all in 1 st, turn, p5, turn, pass 4 of sts just made, 1 at a time, over end st, k tbl.

 k on RS, p on WS   p on RS, k on WS   k2tog   skpo   p2tog   k3tog   sk2po   yo   c2fp

Stitch 198
Leafy vine LEVEL ❸

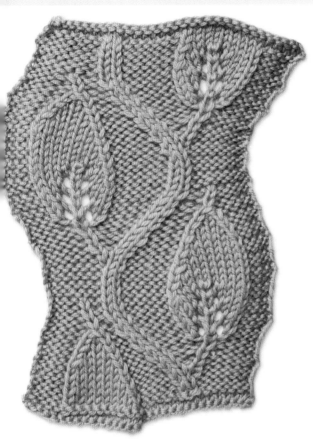

The graceful waving vine stem is made with easy-to-work three-stitch cables on a reverse-stockinette-stitch background. Using separate charts for the leaves avoids having to distort the main chart. If you're repeating this panel, or combining it with other patterns, such as a rope cable, allow extra stitches in reverse stockinette stitch at each side between the panels.

Note

Work leaf A as indicated on the left of the main chart, and leaf B as indicated on the right of the main chart. Note that when casting on, row nine of leaf A represents ten stitches.

Leaf A

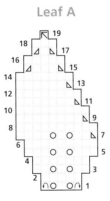

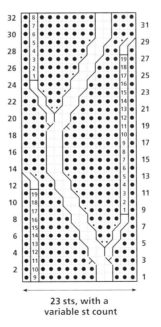

23 sts, with a variable st count

Leaf B

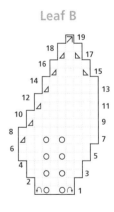

c2bp   c3b   c3bp   c3f   c3fp   m1R   m1L

Stitch 199
Lime leaf LEVEL ❸

Stitch 200
Flame leaves LEVEL ❸

These leaves, looking rather like candle flames, flow into each other in a very rhythmic way. Because of the half-drop repeat pattern, the first row begins with alternate part leaves, but once the logic of gaining and losing stitches is established, the pattern is quite easy to follow.

It requires a surprising number of different increases and decreases to create this modest heart-shaped leaf, but the result is very pretty.

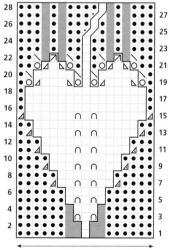

Motif of 13 sts, with a variable st count

Specific symbols

◹ K tbl on WS
◸ Sk2po on WS

Note
A cable needle is required.

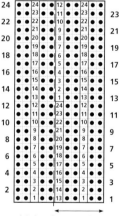

Multiple of 12 sts plus 5, with a variable st count

Note

Work the leaf chart over one stitch and twenty-four rows, as shown on the main chart. When casting on, row thirteen of the leaf chart represents seven stitches (five stitches plus the two stitches knit together in the decrease).

Leaf

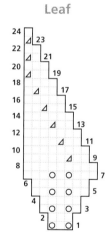

 k on RS, p on WS p on RS, k on WS k2tog skpo p2tog ⋏ s2kpo ⋂ m1 ○ yo ▨ no st

Stitch 201
Embellished cable   LEVEL ❸

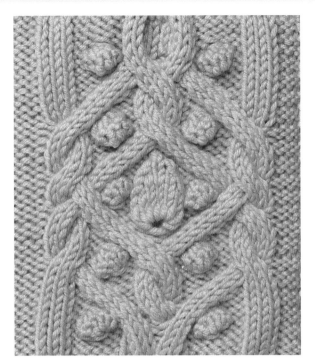

Bobbles enliven the reverse-stockinette-stitch areas of this classic braided cable panel, and a bell decorates the center diamond.

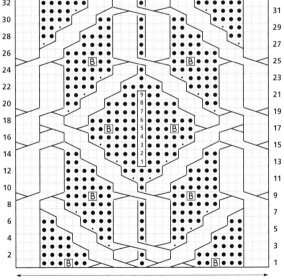

Panel of 31 sts, with a variable st count

Specific symbols

⟨⟩ Sl3 to 1st cable needle, hold at front, sl next st to 2nd cable needle, hold at back, k3, then p1 from 2nd cable needle, then k3 from 1st cable needle.

B (K1, yo, k1, yo, k1) all in 1 st, turn, [k5, turn] twice, pass 4 of sts just made, 1 st at a time, over end st.

Notes

• Work bell chart over one stitch and nine rows, as shown in the center of the diamond on the main chart.

• Two cable needles are required.

Bell

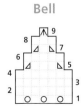

c2bp   c5bp   c5fp   c6b   c6f

Stitch 202
Plume LEVEL ❸

Single increases and a large multiple increase raise this curvy, dimpled motif from its background of reverse stockinette stitch. It could also be used as part of a repeat pattern.

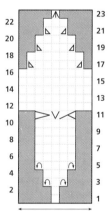

Motif of 1 st, with a variable st count

Specific symbol

⟫∨⟪ Sl3 to cable needle, hold at back, k2, sl nearest st from cable needle back to L needle, (k1, yo, k1, yo, k1) all in this st, k2 rem sts from cable needle.

Notes

• The motif starts with one stitch, increases to nine stitches, and then returns to one stitch on the last row.

• A cable needle is required.

Stitch 203
Leaf within a diamond LEVEL ❸

Leaves, bobbles, and cables make a very flamboyant panel that owes something to the Aran tradition, but remains quite individual.

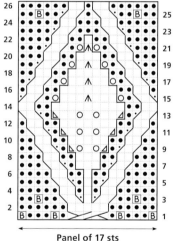

Panel of 17 sts

Specific symbols

B (K1, p1, k1, p1, k1) all in 1 st, turn, p5, turn, k5, turn, p5, turn, sl4 of sts just made, 1 at a time, over end st, then k tbl.

⟫⟪ Sl3 to cable needle, hold at back, k2, sl nearest st on cable needle back to L needle, k this st, k2 rem sts from cable needle.

Note

A cable needle is required.

 □ k on RS, p on WS ● p on RS, k on WS ⧄ k2tog ⧅ skpo ⋀ s2kpo ○ yo ⋂ m1L ⋒ m1R ▨ no st ⟫⟪ c2b

Stitch 204
Bunch of grapes LEVEL ❸

A large group of bobbles contrasts with delicate leaves to suggest fruit of the vine.

Stitch 205
Leaves and berries LEVEL ❸

Highly embossed leaves and bobbles help to give a swinging movement to the branches and stem of this knitted design.

Notes

• Work leaf charts over one stitch and fourteen rows, as shown on right and left of the main chart.

• A cable needle is required.

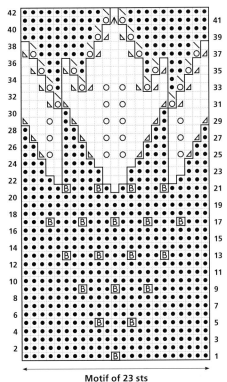

Motif of 23 sts

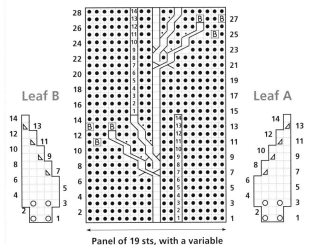

Leaf B

Leaf A

Panel of 19 sts, with a variable st count

Specific symbols

B (K1, p1, k1, p1, k1) all in 1 st, turn, p5, turn, sl4 of sts just made, 1 at a time, over end st, k tbl.

⧄ Sl1 to cable needle, hold at front, k1, p1, then k1 from cable needle.

⧄ Sl2 to cable needle, hold at back, k1, then p1, k1 from cable needle.

⧄ Sl2 to cable needle, hold at back, k1, then p2 from cable needle.

⧄ Sl1 to cable needle, hold at front, p2, then k1 from cable needle.

Specific symbols

B (K1, yo, k1, yo, k1) all in 1 st, turn, p5, turn, k5, turn, p5, turn, sl4 of sts just made, 1 at a time, over end st, k tbl.

◺ K tbl on WS.

⧄c2fp ⧄c2f ⧄c2bp ⧄c3bp ⧄c3fp

STITCH SELECTOR Stranded and Intarsia

Patterning with color in stockinette stitch has a long global history.
So some of these designs—such as Fair Isle—are influenced by
tradition. Some are based on other textiles from the past, and a
few are simply pictorial.

206 Blue bow

207 Rosebud

208 Crab

209 Folded ribbon

210 Kilim border

211 Kilim star

212 Diagonal diamonds

213 Spots

214 Sampler

215 Peerie patterns

216 Little flower and waves

217 Folk bluebells

218 Art nouveau lily

219 Mexican stripes

220 Brocade

221 Shetland star

222 Shaded chevrons

223 Carpet borders

224 Japanese stencil flowers

225 Flowers and waves

226 Daisies

227 Carpet leaves

228 Scroll borders

229 Diagonal triangles

230 Indian borders

231 Paisley with flowers

232 South American kite patterns

233 Celtic border

234 Counterchange

235 Celtic knot motif

236 Snowflake

237 African stars

238 Faith, hope, and charity

Stitch 206
Blue bow LEVEL ❶

Being completely symmetrical, this small design makes a good introduction to intarsia. Some stranding is used, but the main areas are better worked with separate lengths of yarn.

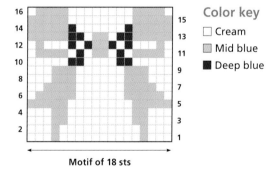

Motif of 18 sts

Color key
☐ Cream
▨ Mid blue
■ Deep blue

Stitch 207
Rosebud LEVEL ❷

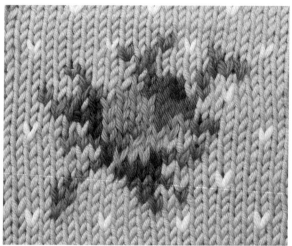

Taken from a vintage textile print, this small rosebud requires naturalistic coloring, although the background colors could be changed. It's a mixture of intarsia and stranded techniques.

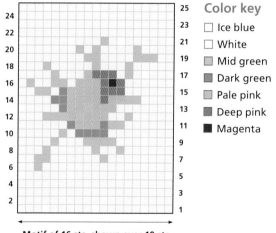

Motif of 16 sts, shown over 19 sts

Color key
☐ Ice blue
☐ White
▨ Mid green
▦ Dark green
▨ Pale pink
▨ Deep pink
■ Magenta

☐ k on RS, p on WS in colors as shown

Stitch 208
Crab LEVEL ❷

Fresh from the seashore, an orange crab makes an amusing intarsia motif with a little stranding included. The motif is symmetrical up to the claws, after which the chart should be followed carefully.

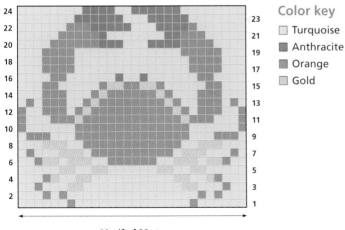

Motif of 28 sts

Color key

- ☐ Turquoise
- ■ Anthracite
- ■ Orange
- ☐ Gold

Stitch 209
Folded ribbon LEVEL ❷

Two geometric shapes create an optical illusion if the diamond is a deeper shade than the lozenge. The colors can be varied endlessly. This is simple stranded knitting, but using three colors at a time.

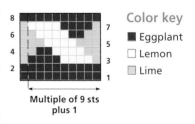

Multiple of 9 sts plus 1

Color key

- ■ Eggplant
- ☐ Lemon
- ☐ Lime

Note

Only one colorway is shown on the chart.

Stitch 210
Kilim border   LEVEL ❷

Shown here as a border, this flower design could also be used as an allover repeat or combined with texture stitches. The stranded knitting is simple and geometric, although four rows use three colors, rather than two.

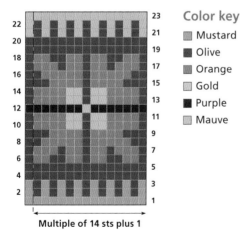

Multiple of 14 sts plus 1

Color key
■ Mustard
■ Olive
■ Orange
□ Gold
■ Purple
□ Mauve

Stitch 211
Kilim star   LEVEL ❷

Shading with a selection of vegetable-dye colors gives this angular star its impact. It's mainly intarsia technique, with a little stranding.

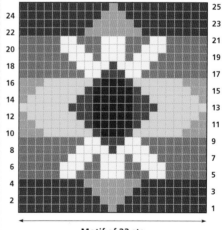

Motif of 23 sts

Color key
■ Plum   □ Pale yellow
▨ Dusky pink   ▨ Mauve
□ Pale green   ■ Eggplant
▨ Mustard   ■ Red brown

134–135 Basic symbols

☐ k on RS, p on WS in colors as shown

Stitch 212
Diagonal diamonds LEVEL ❷

These diagonal color sequences mean that a lot of colors can be introduced in the first row and then carried up the work without leaving many short ends. To add even more color, some of the outside stitches of the diamonds have been embellished with duplicate stitch.

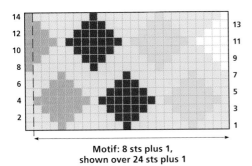

Motif: 8 sts plus 1,
shown over 24 sts plus 1

Color key

☐ Khaki
▨ Mauve
■ Magenta
☐ Turquoise
☐ Lemon

Stitch 213
Spots LEVEL ❸

These concentric circles of color owe something to the Russian Futurists of the twentieth century but look lively and contemporary today. They are best worked entirely in intarsia technique.

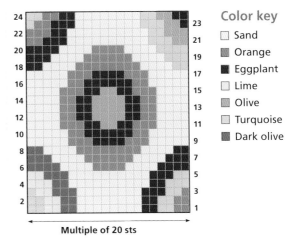

Multiple of 20 sts

Color key

☐ Sand
▨ Orange
■ Eggplant
☐ Lime
▨ Olive
☐ Turquoise
■ Dark olive

Note
The chart shows the stitch repeat but not the color repeat because colors vary from one spot to the next.

Stitch 214

Sampler

LEVEL ❶

Numerals straight from an old cross-stitch sampler could be used to mark a significant date. The whole design is simple two-color stranded knitting, but requires careful reading of the chart on wrong-side rows.

Color key

☐ Cream

▨ Green

■ Dark red

▨ Blue

Panel of 28 sts

☐ k on RS, p on WS in colors as shown

Stitch 215
Peerie patterns
LEVEL ①

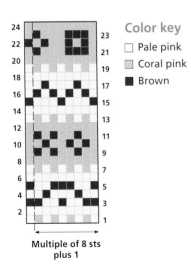

Peerie is a Shetland dialect word meaning "small." This group of classic Shetland patterns can be used together as shown, or the bands can be picked out and alternated with other patterns to create your own design.

Stitch 216
Little flower and waves LEVEL ①

Undulating waves of shaded colors leading in and out of a center motif are a classic device of Shetland patterns. The result is pleasing and very simple to do, since it is straightforward stranded knitting. The waves repeat over four stitches and the flowers over eight stitches.

Stitch 217
Folk bluebells
LEVEL ①

Simple two-color stranded knitting is used to make rows of a folksy flower motif that's inspired by Pennsylvania Dutch stencils.

Color key
- ☐ Pale pink
- ▨ Coral pink
- ■ Brown

Multiple of 8 sts plus 1

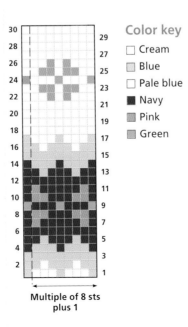

Color key
- ☐ Cream
- ▨ Blue
- ☐ Pale blue
- ■ Navy
- ▨ Pink
- ▨ Green

Multiple of 8 sts plus 1

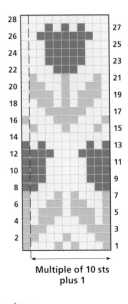

Multiple of 10 sts plus 1

Color key
- ▨ Pale viridian
- ☐ Pale lime
- ■ Mid blue

Stitch 218
Art nouveau lily LEVEL ❷

The swirling lines of this lily-and-leaves design echo the art nouveau style that was all the rage in the 1890s. Although it has a large repeat, the design is mostly in straightforward two-color stranded knitting. The lily bud is worked with a separate length of contrast yarn.

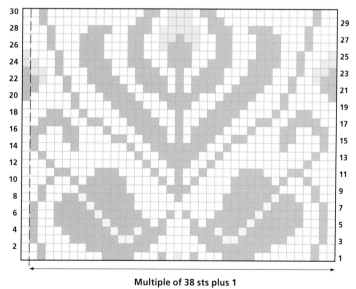

Color key
- ☐ Cream
- ▨ Green
- ☐ Yellow

Multiple of 38 sts plus 1

☐ k on RS, p on WS in colors as shown

Stitch 219
Mexican stripes LEVEL ❶

Bands of simple geometric patterning, alternating between black as the background and black as the motif color, give a vibrant effect, even though it is all just simple two-color stranded knitting.

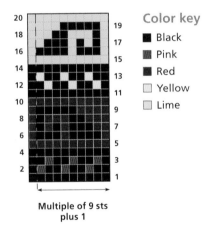

Color key
- ■ Black
- ▨ Pink
- ■ Red
- ☐ Yellow
- ☐ Lime

Multiple of 9 sts
plus 1

Stitch 220
Brocade LEVEL ❶

This type of multiarmed diamond motif is found in embroidery, woven fabrics, and on carpets from eastern Europe and the eastern Mediterranean. Here the motifs combine with a simple diamond to make an allover pattern. The technique is just two-color stranded knitting, so although the repeat is quite large, it is easy to work.

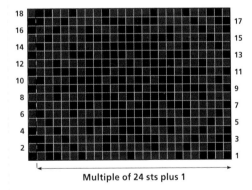

Multiple of 24 sts plus 1

Color key
- ■ Black
- ■ Dark red

Stitch 221
Shetland star LEVEL ❶

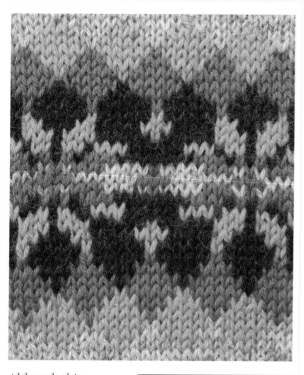

Although this border has a larger repeat than some of the other Shetland patterns, it's all just two-color stranded knitting, so it's just as easy to do. The diamond patterns that shade in and out from the central star motif are called peaks. You could vary the design by adding more peaks in tones of blue.

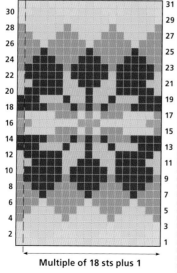

Multiple of 18 sts plus 1

Color key
▨ Natural	■ Brown
▨ Pale blue	▨ Yellow
▨ Blue	▨ Pink

Stitch 222
Shaded chevrons LEVEL ❶

Inspired by bargello embroidery, this design has simple waves of black chevrons on a shaded, striped background. The stripes shade from red through to yellow and back again, but you could play around with different colors or different widths.

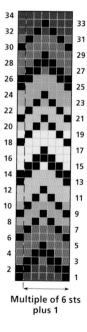

Multiple of 6 sts plus 1

Color key
- ▨ Red
- ■ Black
- ▨ Vermilion
- ▨ Orange
- ▨ Gold
- ☐ Yellow

☐ k on RS, p on WS in colors as shown

Stitch 223
Carpet borders LEVEL ❶

This is based on a Turkish carpet design. With the exception of the center row, all rows are two-color stranded knitting; the center row uses three colors. The pattern bands can be used separately or together. To use them together, you'll need to allow three repeats of the star design to every seven repeats of the pointed borders.

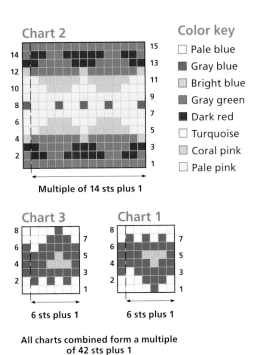

Chart 2

Color key

☐ Pale blue
■ Gray blue
▨ Bright blue
▨ Gray green
■ Dark red
☐ Turquoise
▨ Coral pink
☐ Pale pink

Multiple of 14 sts plus 1

Chart 3   **Chart 1**

6 sts plus 1   6 sts plus 1

All charts combined form a multiple of 42 sts plus 1

Stitch 224
Japanese stencil flowers LEVEL ❸

This design was inspired by a stencil motif with scattered flowers on a spotted background. Working free-flowing motifs with random flecks takes more concentration than working a regular repeat, but only two colors are used so it's not too difficult. When stranding the white yarn over more than four stitches, catch it in with a stitch in the same color in the row below.

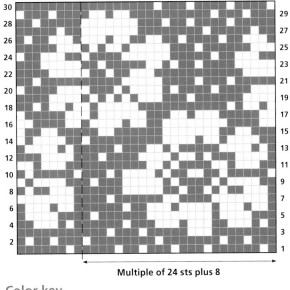

Multiple of 24 sts plus 8

Color key

■ Blue
☐ White

Stitch 225
Flowers and waves LEVEL ②

This design relates to the Shetland waves and flowers, but is given a more contemporary effect by reducing the waves to a simple band and enlarging the flower motif. The chart shows just two colors for the flowers but you could knit each flower in a different color, as shown in the swatch.

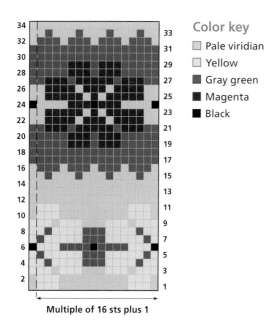

Multiple of 16 sts plus 1

Color key
- ☐ Pale viridian
- ☐ Yellow
- ☐ Gray green
- ☐ Magenta
- ■ Black

Stitch 226
Daisies LEVEL ❸

This flower design echoes the printed fabrics of the 1930s. You'll need to combine intarsia and stranded knitting techniques, using separate lengths of yarn for the flowers, flower centers, and leaves, and carrying the background color behind the motifs.

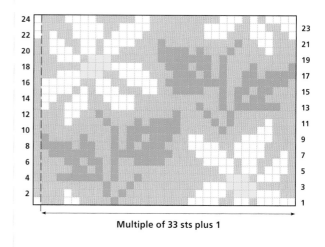

Multiple of 33 sts plus 1

Color key
- ☐ Cream
- ☐ Pale taupe
- ☐ Green
- ☐ Yellow

☐ k on RS, p on WS in colors as shown

Stitch 227
Carpet leaves LEVEL ❸

This design with stylized leaf motifs combines two-color stranded knitting with areas in intarsia. Use separate lengths of yarn for each leaf and for the little chevrons, stranding within each motif but not between motifs.

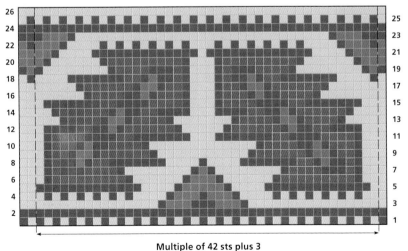

Multiple of 42 sts plus 3

Color key

■ Gray
□ Pale taupe
■ Dark turquoise
■ Burnt orange

Stitch 228
Scroll borders LEVEL ❸

This is a design inspired by carpets from North Africa. Most of the patterns are just two-color stranded knitting, but for the larger center motifs you'll need to use separate lengths of yarn to work the contrast filling in burnt orange.

Color key
■ Black
▨ Burnt orange
▨ Yellow ocher

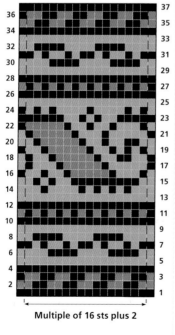

Multiple of 16 sts plus 2

Stitch 229
Diagonal triangles LEVEL ❷

Bright and dark Amish patchwork was the starting point for this pattern. Strand the black background yarn throughout and use separate balls of yarn for each of the contrast triangles. Carrying the contrast yarns diagonally across and up each time a new row of triangles is worked avoids darning in lots of ends.

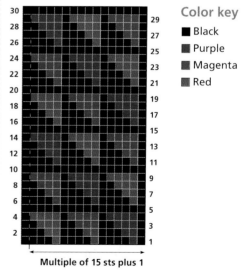

Color key
■ Black
■ Purple
■ Magenta
▨ Red

Multiple of 15 sts plus 1

☐ k on RS, p on WS in colors as shown

Stitch 230
Indian borders LEVEL ❸

Richly decorated Gujarati embroidery was the starting point for this design. While most of the pattern is in two-color stranded knitting, sometimes you'll need to strand three or four colors. For an authentic effect, try mixing shiny and metallic yarns, and accent the design with sequins.

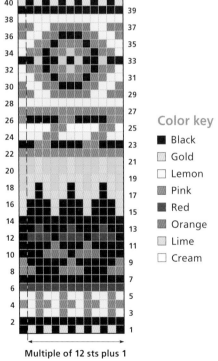

Multiple of 12 sts plus 1

Color key

- ■ Black
- ◻ Gold
- ☐ Lemon
- ▦ Pink
- ■ Red
- ▨ Orange
- ◻ Lime
- ☐ Cream

Stitch 231
Paisley with flowers LEVEL ❸

For this magnificent paisley pattern you'll need to strand the border and the background color, but work the paisley and each flower motif using separate lengths of yarn. For a lively effect, use a different shade of lilac for each flower. If you want just one paisley motif, omit the border and the flowers to give a motif that's thirty stitches wide and forty-seven rows high.

Multiple of 31 sts plus 1

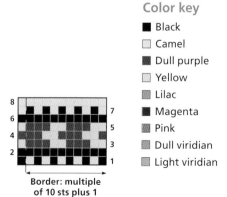

Border: multiple
of 10 sts plus 1

Color key

- ■ Black
- ☐ Camel
- ■ Dull purple
- ☐ Yellow
- ▨ Lilac
- ■ Magenta
- ▨ Pink
- ▨ Dull viridian
- ▨ Light viridian

☐ k on RS, p on WS in colors as shown

Stitch 232
South American kite patterns LEVEL ❸

These bands of pattern were inspired by the vivid geometric designs on the giant kites flown on special occasions in the Andes. You'll need to mix intarsia with stranded color knitting to create this complex design. To add variety, you could vary the shades of each of the colors.

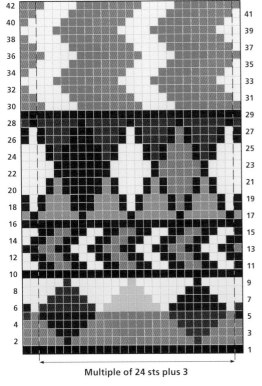

Multiple of 24 sts plus 3

Color key

■ Black
▨ Pink
■ Red
■ Dark turquoise
■ Purple
□ Yellow
▨ Lime
□ Pale lime

Stitch 233
Celtic border LEVEL ②

This border interprets the kind of intertwined knots found on stone crosses. Although it is a large repeat, it's easy to do, since it is all just two-color stranded knitting. The design includes a finishing link at each end. For a continuous border, work just the twenty-eight stitches of the repeat, plus the one stitch to the right.

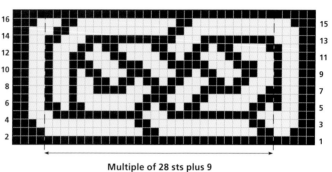

Multiple of 28 sts plus 9

Color key
- ■ Black
- □ Cream

Stitch 234
Counterchange LEVEL ②

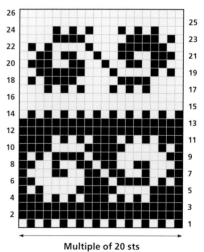

Multiple of 20 sts

Color key
- □ Cream
- ■ Black

Reversing black and white to white and black is a well-known decorative device. Here it adds sparkle to a South American design in stranded knitting.

□ k on RS, p on WS in colors as shown

Stitch 235
Celtic knot motif   LEVEL ❷

This grand knot motif was also inspired by stone crosses. It's just two-color stranded knitting, so although it is big, it's not difficult to do. Surround it with cables that echo the knot for a truly Celtic effect.

Color key

- ■ Black
- □ Cream

Motif of 36 sts

Stitch 236
Snowflake LEVEL ❷

This large Scandinavian-style snowflake is shown with related borders below and a repeat pattern above, but it could be isolated as a motif equally well. It's entirely two-color stranded knitting.

Color key
- ■ Black
- ☐ Cream
- ▦ Red

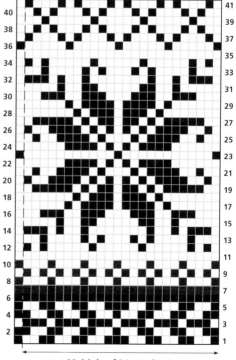

Multiple of 24 sts plus 1

☐ k on RS, p on WS in colors as shown

Stitch 237
African stars LEVEL ❷

Although this design was inspired by an African mud cloth pattern, the way the stars are built up from triangles relates to the stars in the carpet borders design (see page 141). Although it's a large repeat, the pattern is two-color stranded knitting.

Stitch 238
Faith, hope, and charity LEVEL ❷

Allover mesh designs are characteristic of Fair Isle and Scandinavian stranded color knitting. In this variation, rows of diamonds have been filled with crosses (faith), anchors (hope), and hearts (charity). They could be used to decorate the yoke of a fisherman-style sweater.

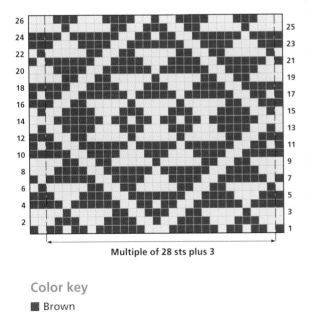

Multiple of 28 sts plus 3

Color key
■ Brown
□ Natural

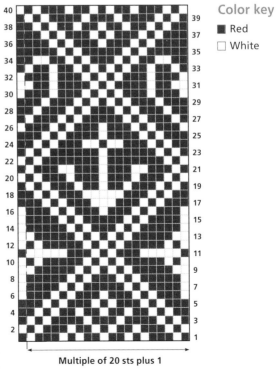

Multiple of 20 sts plus 1

Color key
■ Red
□ White

STITCH SELECTOR Unusual Stitches

This miscellany of curious stitches and techniques offers a starting point for anyone wanting to experiment. You can have fun adapting these techniques to all kinds of applications from clothes and accessories to toys and cushions.

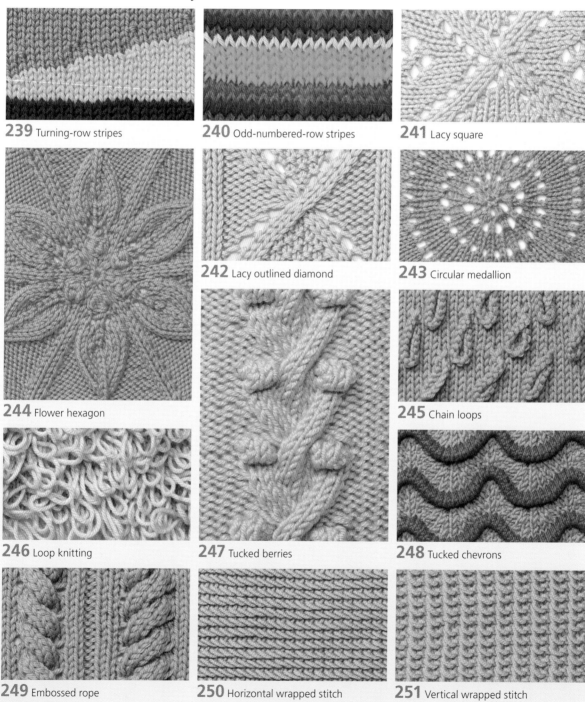

239 Turning-row stripes

240 Odd-numbered-row stripes

241 Lacy square

242 Lacy outlined diamond

243 Circular medallion

244 Flower hexagon

245 Chain loops

246 Loop knitting

247 Tucked berries

248 Tucked chevrons

249 Embossed rope

250 Horizontal wrapped stitch

251 Vertical wrapped stitch

252 Broken stripes

253 Fisherman's rib

254 Two-color fisherman's rib

255 Beaded rib

256 Decorative patch

257 Simple check

258 Sequin spots

259 Slip stitch check

260 Windowpane check

261 Reversible checks

262 Two-color double fabric

263 Postage stamp entrelac

264 Garter stitch entrelac

Stitch 239
Turning-row stripes
LEVEL ❶

There are various ways to make zigzag stripes with turning rows (also called short rows). One method is to turn mid-row and then slip the first stitch of the return row, leaving a small hole at the turn. Wrapping the yarn around a stitch at the turn avoids the hole, but leaves a small blip in the stockinette stitch fabric. Turned stripes can be regular or random.

Method

In the swatch, the stripes are turned at 6-st intervals over 30 sts.

1st row (RS) With A, k.

2nd row P.

3rd and 4th rows K24, wrap, turn, p to end.

5th and 6th rows K18, wrap, turn, p to end.

7th and 8th rows K12, wrap, turn, p to end.

9th and 10th rows K6, wrap, turn, p to end.

11th row K.

12th row With B, p.

13th row K.

14th and 15th rows P6, wrap, turn, k to end.

16th and 17th rows P12, wrap, turn, k to end.

18th and 19th rows P18, wrap, turn, k to end.

20th and 21st rows P24, wrap, turn, k to end.

22nd row P.

These 22 rows form the pattern, varying colors A and B.

Note

To make a wrap, take the yarn between the needles to the opposite side of the work, slip one stitch purlwise, return the yarn to the original side of the work, slip the slipped stitch back on to the left needle and turn, ready to start the short row. This is the same method for both knit and purl rows.

Color key

☐ A

▨ B

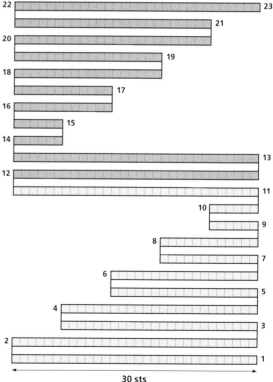

30 sts

☐ k on RS, p on WS   ◩ k2tog   ◨ skpo   Ⓞ yo

Stitch 240
Odd-numbered-row stripes LEVEL ❶

Stockinette-stitch stripes with an odd number of rows tend to leave many ends along the edge where the yarn has to be broken because it can't be carried up the side. However, if you use double-pointed needles instead of conventional ones, you can avoid this problem.

Method

Using double-pointed needles, work your stripe sequence in the usual way, knitting one row and purling the next. When the next row requires a color that is at the opposite end, simply slide the stitches along the needle and knit or purl the row from that end.

Note

This nine-row repeat uses the sliding method, so that all colors are carried up the side. The same technique can be used for random stripes.

Stitch 241
Lacy square LEVEL ❷

This square shows the difference between the yarn overs used as increases to shape the square and the yarn overs used decoratively, which always have a compensatory decrease next to them. Casting on with a crochet hook gives a neat center.

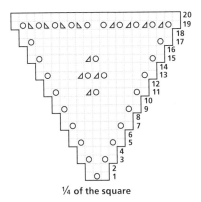

¼ of the square

Notes

- The square is worked in the round with the right side facing, so every row of the chart is read from right to left.
- Use five double-pointed needles.
- To begin, leaving a short end, wind yarn around the left forefinger to form a ring. Using a crochet hook about two sizes smaller than your needles, * insert the hook into the ring and pull a loop through, catch the yarn and pull through the loop on the hook *, slide the ring off your finger and repeat from * to * seven more times to make eight loops on the hook, pull the short end to close the ring, and transfer two stitches to each of four needles.
- To bind off, bring the yarn to the front, slip the first stitch of the round onto the fourth needle, take the yarn to the back, return the stitch to the first needle, turn, and bind off knitwise with the wrong side facing.

Stitch 242
Lacy outlined diamond LEVEL ❷

Stitch 243
Circular medallion LEVEL ❷

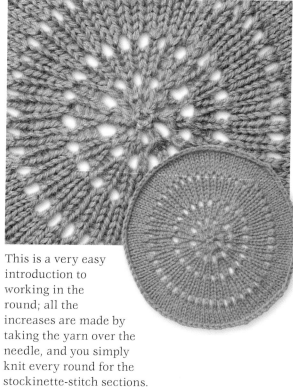

This panel looks like a classic cable diamond pattern. However, the stitches that outline the seed stitch use yarn-over increases and paired decreases to move the stitches, giving the effect of a cable without the work. The only place you'll need a cable needle is for the cross on row twenty-one.

This is a very easy introduction to working in the round; all the increases are made by taking the yarn over the needle, and you simply knit every round for the stockinette-stitch sections.

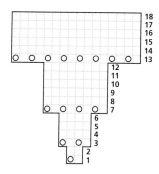

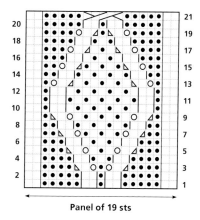

Panel of 19 sts

⅙ of medallion

Specific symbol
Sl3 to cable needle, hold at back, k2, sl nearest st on cable needle to L needle, hold cable needle at front, p1, then k2 from cable needle.

Notes
• Rows two to twenty one form the repeat.
• A cable needle is required.

Notes
• Use four double-pointed needles.
• The medallion is worked in the round with the right side facing, so every row of the chart is read from right to left.
• To begin, cast on two stitches on each of the three needles. To join in a round, bring the yarn to the front, slip the first cast-on stitch onto the third needle, take the yarn to the back, return the stitch to the first needle, turn.

☐ k on RS, p on WS   ● p on RS, k on WS   ◩ k2tog   ◪ skpo   ⚠ s2kpo   ◯ yo

Stitch 244
Flower hexagon LEVEL ❸

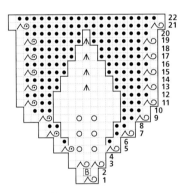

This design uses bobbles and petal motifs. The hexagon is shaped by increases, made by knitting twice into one stitch at the start and purling twice into one stitch at the end of each section.

Specific symbols

⟋⟍◯ K into front and back of st.

⟋⟍◯ P into front and back of st.

B (K1, yo, k1, yo, k1) all in one st, turn, p5, turn, k5, pass 4 of sts just made over end st.

⅙ of the hexagon

Notes
• Use a set of four double-pointed needles.
• The hexagon is worked in the round with the right side facing. Read every row of the chart from right to left.
• To begin, using a crochet hook, make twelve stitches in the same way as the lacy square (see page 55), then transfer four stitches onto each of three needles.
• Work each row of the chart twice for each needle.
• To bind off, bring the yarn in front, slip the first stitch of the round onto the fourth needle, take the yarn to back, return the stitch to the first needle, turn, and bind off knitwise with wrong side facing.

Stitch 245
Chain loops LEVEL ❷

Here decorative loops of chain are placed at regular intervals on a stockinette-stitch background. You'll soon see how you could make a chain loop of any length on any stitch on a right-side row. Place shorter loops closer together for an astrakhan fur effect, work a few rows of longer loops for a fringe, or use individual chain loops to fasten buttons.

Specific symbol

L Insert crochet hook into next st on L needle, pull loop through leaving st on L needle, make 14 more chain sts, insert hook in same st on L needle and pull loop through st and last chain on hook, sl this chain to R needle.

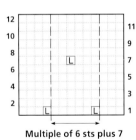

Multiple of 6 sts plus 7

Notes
• A crochet hook about two sizes smaller than the needles is required for the chain loops.
• The chain can be made with knitting needles: [K1, s1 to L needle], then repeat. A crocheted chain is neater and firmer.

Stitch 246
Loop knitting
LEVEL ②

This method of making a fun fur fabric has single loops that are made on the right side of a stockinette-stitch fabric. You can work just a few rows of loops for a fringe, place them on every stitch for a thicker fabric, space them farther apart for a less dense effect, or change colors for a striped loop fabric. The loops are so firm that you can cut them if you want to.

Method

Multiple of 2 sts plus 3.
1st row (RS) K1, [* k next st but do not allow st to drop off L needle, bring yarn between needles to front of work, wind yarn clockwise around left thumb and take it back between needles, k same st and allow st to drop off L needle, return 2 sts just made to L needle and k2tog tbl *, k1] to end.
2nd and 4th rows P.
3rd row K2, [work from * to * of 1st row, k1] to last st, k1.
These 4 rows form the pattern.

Note

Loops can be made smaller or larger depending on how tightly, or even how many times you wind the yarn around your thumb.

Stitch 247
Tucked berries
LEVEL ②

The berries in this pattern may look like bobbles, but they are tiny three-stitch tucks. They have a neat, square appearance that is complemented by a sturdy, branching cable.

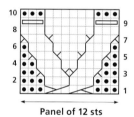

Panel of 12 sts

Specific symbols

▭ [K3, turn, p3, turn] 3 times, fold strip just made to WS, * insert needle in 1st st on L needle, then in back loop of corresponding st of last row before turning rows, k both sts tog; repeat from * twice.

Sl1 to cable needle, hold at back, k3, then k1 from cable needle.

Sl3 to cable needle, hold at front, k1, then k3 from cable needle.

Note

A cable needle is required.

Stitch 248
Tucked chevrons
LEVEL ②

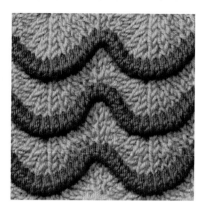

The chevron-patterned background causes these tucks to form smooth waves and makes a decorative edge at the top and bottom. The tucks themselves are six-row stripes, folded and caught up along the row.

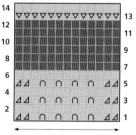

Multiple of 13 sts

Color key
▨ A
▦ B

Specific symbol

▽ With A, k tog st on needle with back loop of corresponding st of 6th row.

☐ k on RS, p on WS   ● p on RS, k on WS   ⬗ k2tog   ⬛ c6b   ⋒ m1

Stitch 249
Embossed rope
LEVEL ❸

These round, three-dimensional ropes are made by an unusual cabling method. Each twist is a loop knitted with short rows.

Right-twist rope

Panel of 12 sts.

1st row (WS) P.

2nd row K10, [turn, p4, turn, k4] 3 times, sl these 4 sts to cable needle, hold at front; take yarn between needles to back, sl4 from R needle to L needle, k6.

3rd row P6, p4 from cable needle, p2.

4th row K.

These 4 rows form the pattern.

Left-twist rope

Panel of 12 sts.

1st row (WS) P.

2nd row K6, [turn, p4, turn, k4] 3 times, sl these 4 sts to cable needle, hold at front; take yarn between needles to back, sl4 from L needle to R needle, k2.

3rd row P2, p4 from cable needle, p6.

4th row K.

These 4 rows form the pattern.

Notes

- Each panel is one eight-stitch rope with two stitches of stockinette stitch at each side.
- One cable needle is required for each rope.

Stitch 250
Horizontal wrapped stitch LEVEL ❷

Although this is based on garter stitch, it's more like another way of knitting, rather than a stitch pattern. The right side has an attractive corded surface, the wrong side looks like reverse stockinette stitch, and the fabric is very firm and stable.

Method

1st row (WS) [Sl1 knitwise, yo] to end.

2nd row [K yo and sl tog tbl] to end.

These 2 rows form the pattern.

Notes

- Can be worked over any number of stitches.
- Keep the wraps fairly loose, but even.
- Take care not to lose the yarn over at the end of the first row when turning for the second row.
- When working the second row, each yarn over should cross over in front of the slipped stitch, insert the right needle through the back of both the yarn over and stitch to knit them together.

Stitch 251
Vertical wrapped stitch LEVEL ❷

Here's another variation on garter stitch with a wrap. Once you get into the flow of wrapping and working stitches together, it's quite easy to do.

Method

Multiple of 2 sts plus 1.

1st row (WS) K1, [yo, sl1 purlwise wyab, k1] to end.

2nd row K1, [k2tog tbl, k1] to end

These 2 rows form the pattern.

Note

Make sure that you take the slipped stitch and the yarn over together when you work the knit two together through the back loop.

Stitch 252
Broken stripes
LEVEL ❶

The subtle stripes are made by alternating knit and purl garter stitch. When you turn the fabric over, you'll see that the stripes are broken in the reverse order. Once you've worked this stitch pattern, you'll see how you could vary the width of the stripes.

Method
Multiple of 8 sts plus 4.
Cast on using A.
1st (RS) and 2nd rows Using A, k4, [p4, k4] to end.
3rd and 4th rows Using B, work as 1st and 2nd rows.
These 4 rows form the pattern.

Note
For the sample swatch, A is blue and B is yellow.

Stitch 253
Fisherman's rib
LEVEL ❷

Knit one, purl one rib is the basis for this version of fisherman's rib. Knitting in the row below is easy; simply insert the right needle into the stitch below the first stitch on the left needle, knit the stitch, which will automatically catch the stitch in the row above, and allow the two stitches to drop off the left needle together.

Method
Multiple of 2 sts plus 3.
1st row (RS) P1, [k1, p1] to end.
2nd row K1, [p1, k1] to end.
These 2 rows are foundation rows and are not repeated.
3rd row Sl1 purlwise, [k1b, p1] to end.
4th row Sl1 knitwise, p1, [k1b, p1] to last st, k1.
Rows 3–4 form the pattern.

Note
Pull tightly on the edge stitches to keep them neat.

Stitch 254
Two-color fisherman's rib LEVEL ❷

This version of fisherman's rib (stitch 253) gives vertical stripes in alternating colors. It's hard to see how the pattern will look, but after you have worked a couple of repeats, tug on the lower edge and it will become clear.

Method
Multiple of 2 sts plus 1.
Cast on using A.
1st row P1, [k1, p1] to end, slide.
This row is a foundation row and is not repeated.
1st row Using B, p1, [k1b, p1] to end, turn.
2nd row Using A, [k1b, p1] to last st, k1b, slide.
3rd row Using B, k1, [p1b, k1] to end, turn.
4th row Using A, [p1b, k1] to last st, p1b, slide.
These 4 rows form the pattern.

Notes
• You will need to use two double-pointed needles or a circular needle.
• *Slide* means slide the stitches along the needle so the next row can be worked in the same direction.
• The stitch pattern is clear when contrasting tones are used. In the sample swatch, A is blue and B is cream.

☐ k on RS, p on WS   ⬛ p on RS, k on WS

Stitch 255
Beaded rib
LEVEL ①

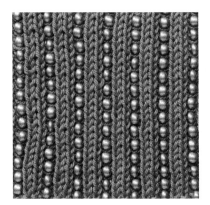

This is the simplest way to add beads to your knitting. Just slide a bead up close so it hangs horizontally between two purl stitches. This method also works well for adding individual larger beads or shaped beads with a hole at the top to a stockinette-stitch fabric. Decide where you want the beads to be placed and work a purl stitch at each side so the bead lies at the front of the fabric.

Method
Multiple of 4 sts plus 2.
1st row (RS) K2, [p1, bead 1, p1, k2] to end.
2nd row P2, [k2, p2] to end.
These 2 rows form the pattern.

Notes
• Thread beads onto the yarn before casting on.
• The easiest way to get the beads onto the yarn is to thread a needle with a short length of sewing thread, knot the ends, and slide the knot up near the eye of the needle. Insert the end of the knitting yarn through the loop of thread, pick up the beads with the point of the needle, and slide them down the loop of thread and onto the yarn.

Stitch 256
Decorative patch
LEVEL ①

No color knitting is needed to create this fun fake patch design. It's simply a square of broken single rib (see page 16) with contrast yarns woven in.

Method
1st row (RS) Using A, p1, [k1, p1] 4 times.
2nd row P.
Repeat these 2 rows 4 times more, and then work 1st row again.

Weaving
Thread tapestry needle with B, knot end, take needle under each p st of 1st rib, tension yarn loosely, knot end, trim and fray ends. Rep along each p rib. Thread wool needle with C, knot end, take needle under each strand of 1st horizontal row of B, knot end, trim and fray as before. Repeat along each remaining row of B.

Notes
• A blunt-pointed tapestry needle is required.
• In the sample swatch, A is gray blue, B is pink, and C is light blue.

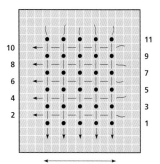

This darned square of broken single rib is 9 sts by 11 rows, but the size can be adjusted

Color key
▦ A

Specific symbols
↓ Direction of B strands.
← Direction of C strands.

Stitch 257
Simple check
LEVEL ①

To create this very effective pattern, work stockinette-stitch stripes then add duplicate stitch to create the checks.

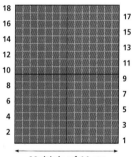

18 17
16 15
14 13
12 11
10   9
 8   7
 6   5
 4   3
 2   1

← Multiple of 14 sts →

Method

Cast on using A (blue).
Beg k, St st 9 rows.
Change to B (pink).
St st 9 rows.
These 18 rows form the stripe pattern.
When the work is the length you require, cast off, then with RS facing, using a tapestry needle, and following the chart, work duplicate stitch with B on the A stripes and with A on the B stripes to create the check pattern.

Note

A blunt-pointed tapestry needle is required to work the duplicate stitch.

Stitch 258
Sequin spots
LEVEL ②

To make the sequins lie flat on the right side of the work, you need to push a sequin through as you knit a stitch. This design places sequins in a regular spot pattern, but you could work them more closely or scatter randomly.

Method

Multiple of 6 sts plus 7.
1st row (RS) K.
2nd row P.
3rd row K.
4th row P.
5th row K3, [sequin 1, k5] to last 4 sts, sequin 1, k3.
6th, 8th, and 10th rows P.
7th and 9th rows K.
11th row K6, [sequin 1, k5] to last st, k1.
12th row P.
These 12 rows form the pattern.

Notes

• Before casting on, thread sequins onto the yarn in the same way as given for beads (see Notes for stitch 255). For larger projects, buy sequins that are already on a strand of nylon thread, which makes it easier to slide them onto the yarn.

• Never press sequins, because this will cause them to curl.

Stitch 259
Slip stitch check
LEVEL ②

This is a three-color pattern, but slipping the stitches creates the checks, so you only ever need to work with one color at a time.

Method

Multiple of 6 sts plus 3.
Cast on with A.
1st row (RS) Using A, k.
2nd row Using B, p3, [sl3 purlwise, p3] to end.
3rd row Using B, k3, [sl3 purlwise, k3] to end.
4th and 5th rows As 2nd and 3rd rows.
6th row Using A, sl3 purlwise, [p3, sl3 purlwise] to end.
7th row Using A, k.
8th row Using C, sl3 purlwise, [p3, sl3 purlwise] to end.
9th row Using C, sl3 purlwise, k3, sl3 purlwise] to end.
10th and 11th rows As 8th and 9th rows.
12th row Using A, p3, [sl3 purlwise, p3] to end.
These 12 rows form the pattern.

Notes

• For this swatch, A is lime green, B is emerald green, and C is cream. When choosing your color scheme, always use the mid tone for A.

• After slipping the stitches, carry the yarn across on the wrong side of the fabric to work the next group of stitches.

☐ k on RS, p on WS   ⬤ p on RS, k on WS

Stitch 260
Windowpane check
LEVEL ❶

To create this very effective pattern, all you do is work a striped rib, then using a crochet hook, fill in the verticals with surface chain.

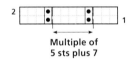

Multiple of
5 sts plus 7

Method
Cast on a multiple of 10 sts plus 7 for these checks.
Cast on using A.
1st row (RS) K3, [p1, k4] to last 4 sts, p1, k3.
2nd row P3, [k1, p4] to last 4 sts, k1, p3.
These 2 rows form the rib pattern as shown on the chart.
Cont in rib, work 3 more rows A, 1 row B, 5 rows C, 1 row D, 5 rows C, 1 row B, 5 rows A, 1 row D.
These 24 rows form the stripe pattern.
When the work is the length you require, bind off. With RS facing, and using crochet hook and alternating B and D, work surface chain up each of the 1-st verticals.

Notes
• A crochet hook is required, two or three sizes smaller than the needles.
• For the sample swatch, A is lime, B is black, C is pink, and D is cream.

Stitch 261
Reversible checks
LEVEL ❷

This double fabric has checks in stockinette stitch on each side. You'll see that the checks are the opposite colors on the front and back.

Method
Worked over a mutiple of 16 sts plus 8.
Cast on using A.
1st line of checks, 1st row Using B, * [wyab, k1, wyif, sl1 purlwise] 4 times, [wyab, sl1 purlwise, wyif, p1] 4 times, rep from * to last 8 sts, [wyab, k1, wyif, sl1 purlwise] 4 times, slide.
2nd row Using A, * [wyab, sl1 purlwise, wyif, p1] 4 times, [wyb, k1, wyif, sl1 purlwise] 4 times, rep from * to last 8 sts, [wyab, sl1 purlwise, wyif, pl] 4 times, turn.
3rd row Using A, work as 1st row.
4th row Using B, work as 2nd row.
5th, 6th, 7th, 8th, 9th, and 10th rows Work 1st to 4th rows again, then work 1st and 2nd rows.
2nd line of checks Work 1st to 10th rows noting that position of checks is reversed.
These 20 rows form the pattern.
To balance the checks, end with a first line of checks.
Preparation for binding off Using A, * [sl1 knitwise] twice, return sts to L needle, noting that the position of the colors in row is reversed, p2tog, rep from * to end. Bind off purlwise.

Notes
• Use two double-pointed needles or a circular needle.
• *Slide* simply means to slide the stitches along the needle so the next row can be worked in the same direction.
• For the sample swatch, A is pink and B is green.
• When changing colors, twist the yarns on the wrong side.

Stitch 262
Two-color double fabric
LEVEL ❶

Stitch 263
Postage stamp entrelac
LEVEL ❸

This ingenious way of knitting makes a reversible fabric that has stockinette stitch in a different color on each side.

Method

Multiple of 2 sts.

Cast on using A.

1st row Using B, [wyab, k1, wyif, sl1 purlwise] to end, slide.

2nd row Using A, [wyab, sl1 purlwise, wyif, p1] to end, turn.

3rd row Using A, work as 1st row.

4th row Using B, work as 2nd row.

These 4 rows form the pattern.

On the row before binding off, using A, work k2tog across the row, then bind off in the usual way.

Notes

- Use a circular needle or two double-pointed needles.
- *Slide* means to slide the stitches along to the other end of the needle so the next row can be worked in the same direction.
- When changing colors, twist the yarns to link the areas.
- In the sample swatch, A is pink and B is green.

Entrelac is a fascinating technique that uses small blocks of knitting, picked up and worked continuously to create a fabric. This version is in stockinette stitch and has really tiny blocks, giving a woven effect.

Notes

- In the sample swatch A is wine and B is pink. If you prefer, you could work the stitch pattern all in one color or in three or more colors.
- When working the lines of blocks, pick up one stitch from every two row ends.
- A small sample can be worked on straight needles, but it is easier to spread out the stitches and see how the blocks interlace if you use a circular needle when working a larger piece such as a cushion or a throw.
- The method is for blocks of four stitches and eight rows, which is probably the smallest practical size, but you could adapt the pattern to be worked on a multiple of any number of stitches to give larger blocks.

Method
Cast on using A. Cont in A.

Base triangles
1st row (RS) K1, turn.
2nd row P1.
3rd row K2, turn.
4th row P2.
5th row K3, turn.
6th row P3.
7th row K4, turn.
8th row P4.
9th row K5, turn.
These 9 rows form 1st base triangle. Row 9 is 1st row of 2nd base triangle. Rep rows 2–9 until required number of base triangles have been completed, ending last triangle k4.

1st line of blocks
Worked into row ends of base triangles. Change to B.
1st side triangle Worked into 4 sts of 1st base triangle.
1st row P1, turn.
2nd row Kfb. 2 sts.
3rd row P1, p2tog, turn.
4th row Sl1 purlwise, kfb. 3 sts.
5th row P2, p2tog, turn.
6th row Sl1 purlwise, k1, kfb. 4 sts.
7th row P3, p2tog, do not turn.
Leave these 4 sts on needle.
1st block Worked into 4 sts of next base triangle.
Pick up and p 4 sts from row ends of first base triangle, turn.
1st row (RS) K4, turn.
2nd row P3, p2tog, turn.
3rd row Sl1 purlwise, k3.
4th row As 2nd row.
Work rows 3–4 two more times, using all sts of base triangle.
Cont in this way, picking up and purling 4 sts from row ends of same base triangle and working into sts of next base triangle until all blocks have been completed.

2nd side triangle Pick up and purl 4 sts from row ends of last base triangle, turn.
1st row (RS) K4, turn.
2nd row P4.
3rd row K2tog, k2. 3 sts.
4th row P3.
5th row K2tog, k1. 2 sts.
6th row P2.
7th row K2tog. Fasten off.
1st line of blocks has been completed.

2nd line of blocks
Worked into 1st line of blocks.
Using A, pick up and k 4 sts from straight row ends of 2nd side triangle, turn.
1st row (WS) P4, turn.
2nd row K3, skpo, turn.
3rd row Sl1 purlwise, p3.
4th row As 2nd.
Work rows 3–4 two more times, using all 4 sts of block.
Cont in this way, picking up and knitting 4 sts from row ends of same block and working into sts of next block until last block. Work last block into sts of 1st side triangle.
2nd line of blocks has been completed.
Alternating colors and working following 1st lines of blocks into 2nd lines of blocks in same way as working into base triangles, rep 1st and 2nd lines of blocks to give required length, ending with a 1st line of blocks.

Closing triangles
Using A, pick up and knit 4 sts from row ends of 2nd side triangle, turn.
1st row (WS) P4.
2nd row K3, skpo, turn.
3rd row Sl1 purlwise, p1, p2tog.
4th row K2, skpo, turn.
5th row Sl1 purlwise, p2tog.
6th row K1, skpo, turn.
7th row P2tog.
8th row Skpo, do not turn.
With 1 st on R needle, pick up and knit 3 sts from row ends of block, turn. 4 sts.
Cont in this way until all closing triangles have been completed. Bind off.

Stitch 264
Garter stitch entrelac LEVEL ❸

Here's a variation on the entrelac technique with the blocks worked in alternate lines of knit garter stitch and purl garter stitch. Because garter stitch has an almost square gauge, the blocks are square and lie flat.

Method

Multiple of 12 sts.
Cast on using A. Cont in A.

Base triangles

1st row (RS) K2tog, turn.
2nd row K1.
3rd row K2, turn.
4th row K2.
5th row K3, turn.
6th row K3.
7th row K3, k2tog, turn.
8th row K4.
9th row K5, turn.
10th row K5.
11th row K6, turn.
12th row K6.
13th row K6, k2tog, turn.
14th row K7.
15th row K8, turn.
16th row K8.
17th row K9, turn.
18th row K9.
19th row K9, k2tog, turn.
Rows 1–18 form 1st base triangle. Row 19 is the 1st row of the 2nd base triangle.
Work rows 2–19 until the last base triangle is reached, then work rows 2–18.
Last row K9.

Notes

• For the sample swatch, A is dark blue and B is light blue. You can use as many colors as you like, and adapt the pattern to work on a smaller or larger multiple of stitches.
• The decreases in the base triangles stop the lower edge from pulling in.

1st line of blocks

Worked into row ends of base triangles. Change to B.

1st side triangle Worked into 9 sts of last base triangle.

1st row (WS) P1, turn.

2nd row P1.

3rd row P2, turn.

4th row P2.

5th row Pfb, p2tog, turn.

6th row P3.

7th row Pfb, p1, p2tog, turn.

8th row P4.

9th row Pfb, p2, p2tog, turn.

10th row P5.

11th row Pfb, p3, p2tog, turn.

12th row P6.

13th row Pfb, p4, p2tog, turn.

14th row P7.

15th row Pfb, p5, p2tog, turn.

16th row P8.

17th row Pfb, p6, p2tog, turn.

18th row P9.

19th row P9, leave these 9 sts on needle.

1st block Pick up and purl 9 sts from row ends of same base triangle, turn.

1st row (RS) P9.

2nd row P8, p2tog, turn.

Work these 2 rows 8 more times, using all sts of base triangle. Leave these 9 sts on needle.

Cont working blocks in this way, picking up and purling 9 sts from row ends of same base triangle and working into next base triangle until all blocks have been completed.

2nd side triangle Pick up and purl 9 sts from row ends of last base triangle, turn.

1st row P9.

2nd row P9.

3rd row P2tog, p7.

4th row P8.

5th row P2tog, p6.

6th row P7.

7th row P2tog, p5.

8th row P6.

9th row P2tog, p4.

10th row P5.

11th row P2tog, p3.

12th row P4.

13th row P2tog, p2.

14th row P3.

15th row P2tog, p1.

16th row P2.

17th row P2tog.

18th row P1.

Bind off.

2nd line of blocks

Worked into 1st line of blocks. Change to A.

Pick up and knit 9 sts from row ends of 2nd side triangle.

1st row (WS) K9.

2nd row K8, skpo, turn.

Work these 2 rows 8 more times, so using all 9 sts of block. Do not turn at end of final row.

Cont in this way picking up and knitting 9 sts from row ends of same block and working into sts of next block, until last block, work last block into sts of 1st side triangle.

Working following 1st lines of blocks into 2nd lines of blocks in same way as working into base triangles, repeat 1st and 2nd lines of blocks to give required length, ending with 1st line of blocks.

Closing triangles

1st closing triangle Pick up and knit 9 sts from row ends of 2nd side triangle, turn.

1st row (WS) K9.

2nd row K8, skpo, turn.

3rd row K7, k2tog.

4th row K7, skpo, turn.

5th row K6, k2tog.

6th row K6, skpo, turn.

7th row K5, k2tog.

8th row K5, skpo, turn.

9th row K4, k2tog.

10th row K4, skpo, turn.

11th row K3, k2tog.

12th row K3, skpo, turn.

13th row K2, k2tog.

14th row K2, skpo, turn.

15th row K1, k2tog.

16th row K1, skpo, turn.

17th row K2tog.

18th row Skpo.

Next closing triangle 1 st on R needle, pick up and knit 9 sts from row ends of next block, turn.

1st row (WS) K8, k2tog.

Work rows 2–18 to complete triangle. Cont in this way until all closing triangles have been completed. Bind off.

STITCH SELECTOR Letters

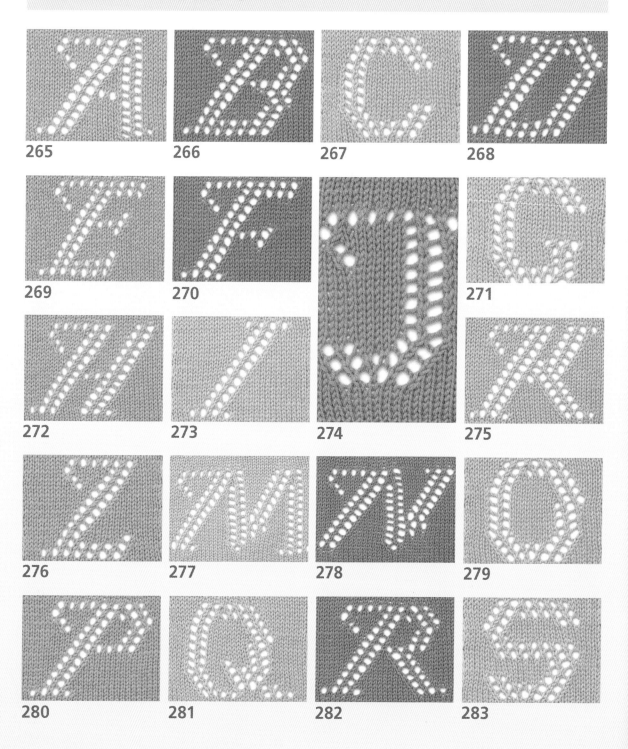

265

266

267

268

269

270

271

272

273

274

275

276

277

278

279

280

281

282

283

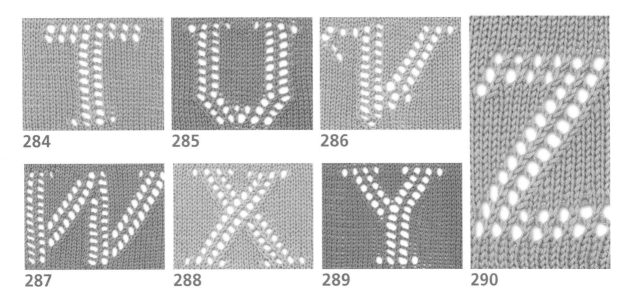

284

285

286

287

288

289

290

STITCH SELECTOR Numbers

291

292

293

294

295

296

297

298

299

300

Stitches 265–269

Letters LEVEL ❷

You can use this delicate alphabet as a sampler, to sign your work, or to make a message. Although the individual letters are easy to work, the fun comes when you decide how to use them. Pick out the letters you want to use and copy them onto graph paper, playing around with the spacing between to get the effect you want.

Note

All letters are twenty-three rows high and vary in width between sixteen and thirty-three stitches.

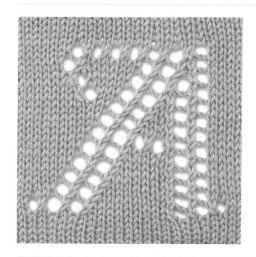

20 sts

22 sts

☐ k on RS, p on WS   ◩ k2tog   ◪ skpo   ◪ k3tog   O yo

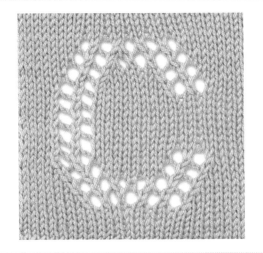

Row numbers (right): 23, 21, 19, 17, 15, 13, 11, 9, 7, 5, 3, 1
Row numbers (left): 22, 20, 18, 16, 14, 12, 10, 8, 6, 4, 2

17 sts

Row numbers (right): 23, 21, 19, 17, 15, 13, 11, 9, 7, 5, 3, 1
Row numbers (left): 22, 20, 18, 16, 14, 12, 10, 8, 6, 4, 2

23 sts

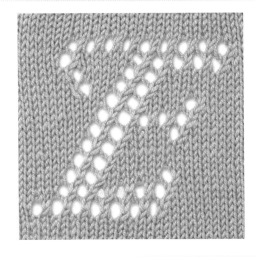

Row numbers (right): 23, 21, 19, 17, 15, 13, 11, 9, 7, 5, 3, 1
Row numbers (left): 22, 20, 18, 16, 14, 12, 10, 8, 6, 4, 2

23 sts

Stitches 270–275

Letters LEVEL ❷

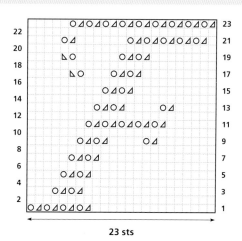

23 sts

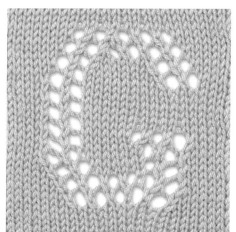

16 sts

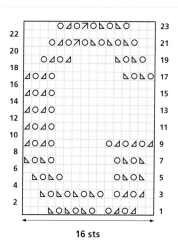

25 sts

172–173 Basic symbols

☐ k on RS, p on WS   ◿ k2tog   ◣ skpo   Ⓞ yo

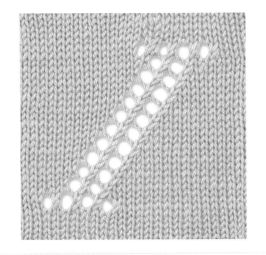

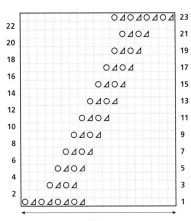

19 sts

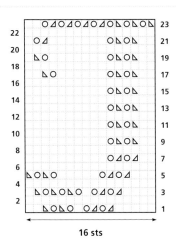

16 sts

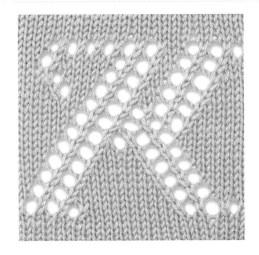

25 sts

Stitches 276–279

Letters LEVEL ❷

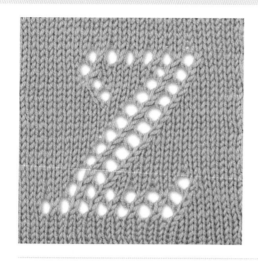

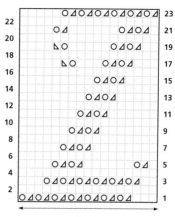

17 sts

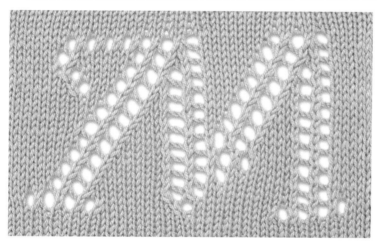

33 sts

☐ k on RS, p on WS   ⬛ k2tog   ◣ skpo   ◥ k3tog   Ⓞ yo

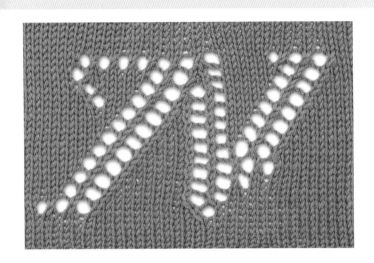

```
22                                                              23
20  O⊿O⊿O⊿O⊿O⊿O⟍O        O⊿O⊿O
18  O⊿              O⊿O⊿⊿O          O⊿O
16  ◣O            O⊿O⟍O⊿O          O⊿O
    ◣O          O⊿O⊿⊿O⊿O          O⊿O    17
14            O⊿O⊿  ⊿O⊿O        O⊿O      15
12          O⊿O⊿    ⊿O⊿O      O⊿O        13
10        O⊿O⊿      ⊿O⊿O    O⊿O          11
8        O⊿O⊿      ⊿O⊿O  O◣O◣          9
6      O⊿O⊿        ⊿O⊿O⊿O⊿O            7
4     O⊿O⊿          ⊿O⊿O⊿O              5
2    O⊿O⊿            ◣O◣O                3
1  O⊿O⊿O⊿                  ◣O            1
```

30 sts

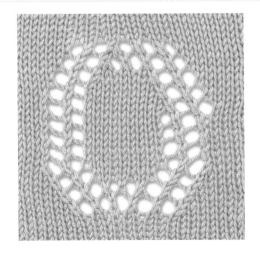

```
22                O⊿O⟍O◣O⊿O            23
20      O⊿O⟍O◣O⊿O◣O⊿O                  21
18        O⊿O⊿          ◣O◣O            19
16    ⊿O⊿O                ◣O◣O          17
14    ⊿O⊿O                  ◣O◣O        15
12    ⊿O⊿O                  O◣O◣        13
10    ⊿O⊿O                  O◣O◣        11
8     ⊿O⊿O                  O◣O◣        9
6     ◣O◣O                    O⊿O⊿      7
4      ◣O◣O                  O⊿O⊿       5
2       ◣O◣O◣O  O⊿O⊿O⊿                  3
1        ◣O◣O  O⊿O⊿O⊿                   1
```

17 sts

Stitches 280–285
Letters LEVEL ❷

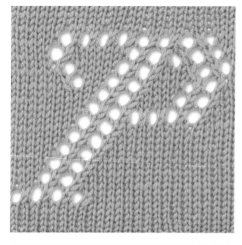

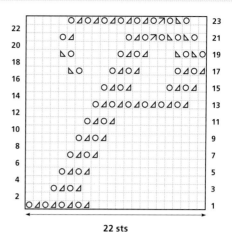

22 sts

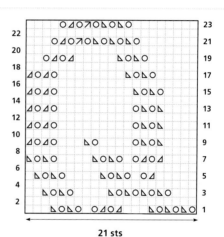

21 sts

23 sts

□ k on RS, p on WS   ◢ k2tog   ◣ skpo   ⌐ k3tog   O yo

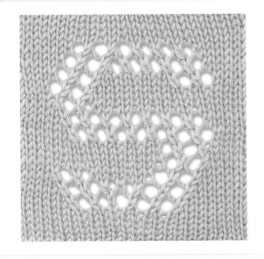

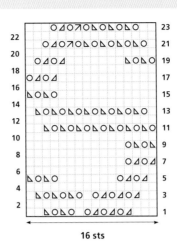

	O	⊿	O	↗	O	⊾	O	⊾	O	⊾	O	⊾	O		23
	O	⊿	O	↗	O	⊾	O	⊾	O	⊾	O	⊾	O		21
	O	⊿	O	⊿						⊾	O	⊾	O		19
O	⊿	O	⊿												17
⊾	O	⊾	O												15
	⊾	O	⊾	O	⊾	O	⊾	O	⊾	O	⊾	O			13
	⊾	O	⊾	O	⊾	O	⊾	O	⊾	O	⊾	O			11
									O	⊾	O	⊿			9
									O	⊿	O	⊿			7
⊾	O	⊾	O					O	⊿	O	⊿				5
	⊾	O	⊾	O			O	⊿	O	⊿	O	⊿			3
	⊾	O	⊾	O			O	⊿	O	⊿	O	⊿			1

16 sts

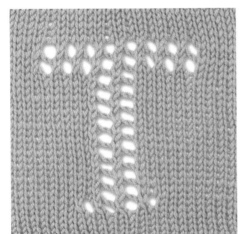

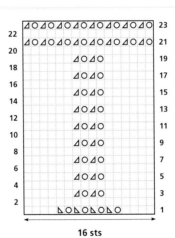

⊿	O	⊿	O	⊿	O	⊿	O	⊿	O	⊿	O	⊿	O		23
⊿	O	⊿	O	⊿	O	⊿	O	⊿	O	⊿	O	⊿	O		21
					⊿	O	⊿	O							19
					⊿	O	⊿	O							17
					⊿	O	⊿	O							15
					⊿	O	⊿	O							13
					⊿	O	⊿	O							11
					⊿	O	⊿	O							9
					⊿	O	⊿	O							7
					⊿	O	⊿	O							5
					⊿	O	⊿	O							3
	⊾	O	⊾	O	⊾	O	⊾	O							1

16 sts

⊿	O	⊿	O	⊿	O	⊿	O					O	⊾	O	⊾	O	⊾	O	⊾		23
⊿	O	⊿	O											O	⊾	O	⊾				21
⊿	O	⊿	O											O	⊾	O	⊾				19
⊿	O	⊿	O											O	⊾	O	⊾				17
⊿	O	⊿	O											O	⊾	O	⊾				15
⊿	O	⊿	O											O	⊾	O	⊾				13
⊿	O	⊿	O											O	⊾	O	⊾				11
⊿	O	⊿	O											O	⊾	O	⊾				9
⊾	O	⊾	O											O	⊿	O	⊿				7
	⊾	O	⊾	O									O	⊿	O	⊿					5
	⊾	O	⊾	O	⊾	O			O	⊿	O	⊿	O	⊿							3
	⊾	O	⊾	O				O	⊿	O	⊿	O	⊿								1

21 sts

Stitches 286–290
Letters LEVEL ❷

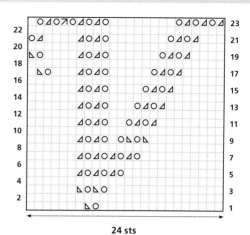

24 sts

33 sts

 k on RS, p on WS k2tog skpo k3tog yo

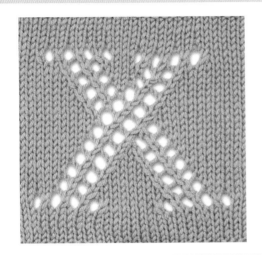

21 sts

21 sts

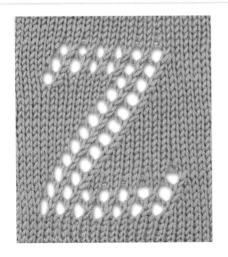

16 sts

Stitches 291–295
Numbers LEVEL ❷

You can use these numbers to date your work or combine them with the letters to make a sampler. The numbers are based on the same lace construction as the letters, but are slimmer and more upright. To create your own combination of numbers, copy them onto graph paper and play around with the spacing to get the effect you want.

Note

All numbers are twenty-three rows high and vary in width between eight and seventeen stitches.

16 sts

8 sts

☐ k on RS, p on WS   ◿ k2tog   ◺ skpo   ▲ s2kpo   ↗ k3tog   O yo

15 sts

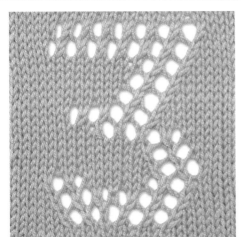

16 sts

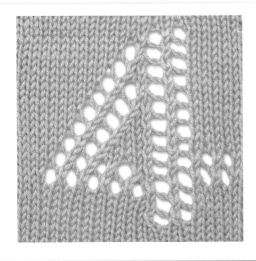

17 sts

Stitches 296–300

Numbers LEVEL ②

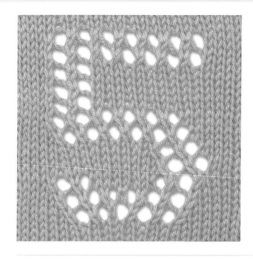
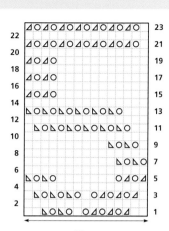

15 sts

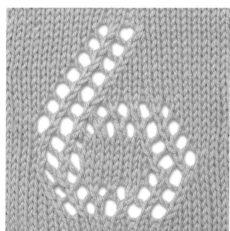
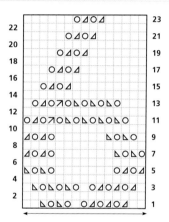

15 sts

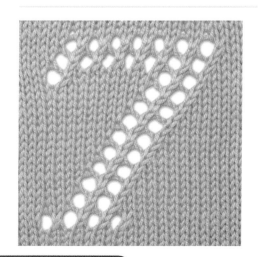
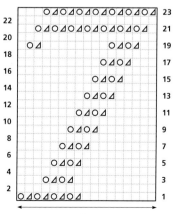

17 sts

☐ k on RS, p on WS ◸ k2tog ◿ skpo ◹ k3tog ○ yo

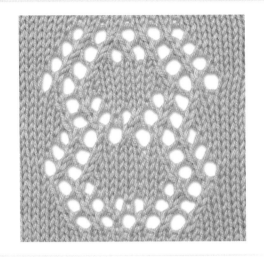

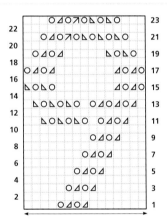

15 sts

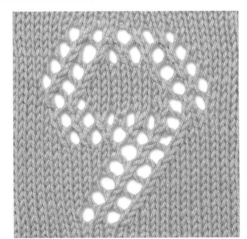

15 sts

Knit
know-how

Turn over to find a wealth of rich information to guide you, including advice on how to incorporate the stitches in the book into your own designs, illustrated essential techniques, key information on how to read the charts, and a list of abbreviations and symbols used in this book.

Using the stitches

If the stitches in this book have inspired you to create your own designs, these pages will show you how. First of all, you need to decide what to make and then make a simple construction drawing. Once you have your measurements and yarn ready, you can start knitting.

HOW TO CREATE YOUR OWN DESIGN

So you know what you want to make, but now you need to plan how to make it. Whatever it is, from a blanket to a hat or a sweater, do a little drawing or a diagram of the design—no matter how basic—and take notes. As the design develops, you may need to adapt or change things, but it helps if you have something to remind you of your original idea. Look at your drawing and consider the construction of your design. For instance, a blanket might be worked in strips or squares, but a hat might be worked in the round or in sections.

Construction and measurements

Whatever it is you are making, draw a diagram of the separate shapes needed, then add measurements to your diagrams. For a garment, you can take measurements directly from the body, then add the amount of roominess you want for the style you are making, or you can take measurements from an existing garment that is similar in style, fit, and weight of fabric to your intended project.

The measurements you take for accessories and household items should cover the width and length, plus movement room, if appropriate. Remember that a knitted fabric is usually stretchy, so cushions will look plumper if the cover is slightly smaller than the cushion pad.

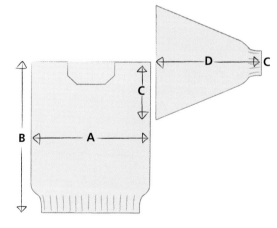

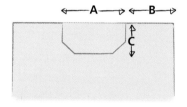

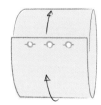

Cushion cover
One of the simplest designs to construct is a cushion cover, because it can be worked in one piece (in the direction of the arrows), with the cast-on and cast-off edges overlapping. Buttonholes near the cast-off edge will provide a fastening for the opening once the side seams have been stitched.

Sweater design: Front
There's no need to draw both sleeves, because they will be the same. The most important measurements are width (A) and length (B). With these proportions in mind, you must plan an armhole depth (C) that gives sufficient movement room. Always measure a sleeve straight (D) and not along the shaped seam edge. With this style it is important to remember to take into account that the top of the sleeve will lie below your natural shoulder. To roughly calculate the sleeve length, take a cuff-to-cuff measurement of yourself—A plus (2 x D)—then subtract A and divide the answer by 2. It's not as complicated as it sounds!

Sweater design: Neck opening
Planning the neck opening is crucial, but if your calculations are wrong, it's not too big a task to reknit at this point. Obviously, the neck must fit over your head, but whatever the style, the relationship of the neck width (A) to the shoulder (B) is important. The depth of the neck (C) will affect both fit and style. Shallow shaping at the back neck will help the neck sit well but isn't absolutely essential. Then there's an edging, neckband, or collar to consider.

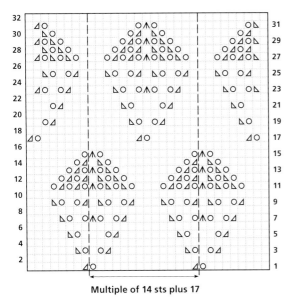

Multiple of 14 sts plus 17

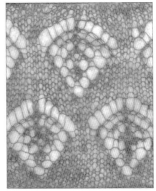 

Yarn differences
These two swatches show how diverse a stitch pattern, in this case Fern lace (see page 99), can look in different yarns. Thick, soft yarn scales up the motif on the right to give a bold effect, while fine mohair makes a delicate, airy fabric and needs more repeats of the pattern to cover the same area.

Start with swatches

Take the yarn of your choice and the needle size that you think is appropriate and knit swatches (samples) in your chosen stitch pattern. You'll need to experiment to create a fabric that you feel is right for your project, so you may need to try out several different needle sizes before you get the effect you want. A firm fabric might be good for a cushion cover but would be too harsh for a baby's garment; a soft fabric will drape well for a cardigan but wouldn't be appropriate for a rugged outdoor pullover. The fiber content and texture of the yarn will also affect the result. A brushed yarn will obscure the stitch pattern if worked tightly, but could look lovely when worked loosely. You can use the information on the ball band as a starting point for choosing which needle size to use, but one of the joys of creating your own designs is that you can work with the needle size that gives you the fabric you like. Always try out all the stitch patterns that you are going to use, either together or separately.

Measuring gauge

Once you are happy with your yarn choice, you will need to measure your swatch to find out how many stitches and rows you have to a given measurement, usually either 4in or 10cm. This is called gauge (tension), and the number of stitches is key to calculating size. If you want a larger or smaller gauge, don't try to knit more loosely or more tightly; simply try a different needle size.

Counting the stitches

With the swatch on a flat surface, place two pins exactly 4in (10cm) apart, as shown in **1**. Count the number of stitches (and any half stitch) along a straight row between the pins. Next place the pins 4in (10cm) apart vertically (as shown in **2**) and count the number of stitches along a straight line between them.

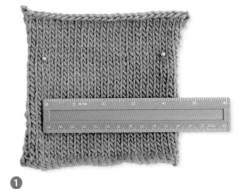

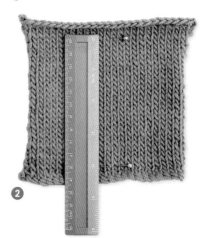

Using the stitches—continued

Working out the numbers

Once your measurements are on your diagram and you've noted the gauge of your swatches, you'll need to connect the two using a calculator. Let's start with a design that uses just one stitch pattern.

If you are working in inches, take the number of stitches in 4in and divide it by 4, then multiply the answer by the number of inches for each width measurement. To establish each length measurement, do the same using the row tension. If you are working in centimeters, take the number of stitches you have in 10cm and divide it by 10, then multiply the answer by the number of centimeters for each width measurement. Do the same using the row tension to work out each of the length measurements.

These calculations will give you an idea of how many stitches you will need, but if necessary, adjust the figures so that you have a stitch count that will give you a total of complete repeats in your chosen stitch pattern.

For a design that combines a background stitch pattern with panels, measure the width of the panels and then calculate the background stitches between. Make sure that any shapings won't break into the pattern in an unattractive way. Don't forget to add any extra stitches that will be lost in seams.

Making row repeats work together
Selecting stitch patterns that will add up to a single row repeat is the most satisfactory way to deal with multiple repeats. In this example, the lace panel crocus (see page 89), a repeat of twenty-four rows, is edged with six four-row repeats of off-center cable (see page 54)— the cable on the right worked as a front cross —and three eight-row repeats of zigzag branch (see page 56) to make a complete stitch pattern of twenty-four rows.

8 rows × 3   4 rows × 6   24 rows × 1   4 rows × 6

24 rows

Shaping in a lace stitch

Increasing or decreasing at a side edge can be tricky, because the shapings can get mixed up with the pattern and ruin the stitch count. This is where charting a design can be very helpful. The illustration shows a shaped edge in harebell (see page 87), with the stitch pattern taken as close to the edge as possible. The chart shows how double decreases have been used to keep the pattern correct and to shape the edge.

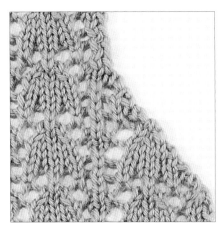

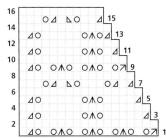

Combining stitch patterns

A combination of cables and twisted rib make an interesting welt (lower edge) pattern that relates beautifully to the jack-in-the-box design (see page 116). The welt cables are worked over five stitches in the same way as the cables used in the main part, and the number of stitches in the twisted rib are the same as the number of stitches in the double moss at the lower part of the lattice.

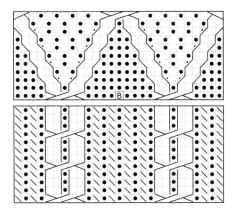

Using the stitches—continued

HOW TO INTEGRATE THE STITCHES INTO YOUR DESIGN

You can create a wealth of fantastic designs by combining stitch patterns, but it's not always as simple as swapping from one stitch to another. Consider combining some patterns that you know well with one or two that you are less familiar with, but look critically at how they interact with each other. Don't be afraid to adjust stitch and row counts for compatibility, or mix stitch patterns with different drape qualities. Bear in mind that the character of the stitch pattern and the fiber content of the yarn (see Yarn differences, page 187) will both affect how the knitted fabric will behave. However, there are various ways you can influence things. A few techniques are shown here, but you can experiment for yourself.

Integrating simple stitch patterns

If you use the same number of stitches for k2, p2 rib, and stockinette stitch, the result will be the contracted rib and expanded stockinette stitch shown in swatch **1**. If this isn't the effect you want, you can make a fabric with continuous width by casting on more stitches and decreasing along the last row of the rib. In swatch **2**, on the right side, the knit stitches of the last row of the rib were worked k2tog. If fewer decreases are required, the decreases could be worked along the first row of stockinette stitch.

Working diagonally

Garter-stitch squares needn't be knitted from side to side; they can be worked from corner to corner, as shown in the instructions given below. This has the advantage that all the edges are exactly the same measurement.

Cast on 1 st.
1st row: (RS) (K1, p1, k1) all in 1 st to make 3 sts.
2nd and WS rows: K.
3rd row: Kfb twice, k1. 5 sts.
5th row: Kfb, k2, kfb, k1. 7 sts. Cont to increase in 1st and last but 1 st on RS rows until the edges are of the required length.
Next RS row: K2tog, k to last 2 sts, skpo. Continue to decrease in this way until 3 sts remain.
Next RS row: Skpo. Fasten off.

Controlling cast-on and cast-off edges

Stitches such as cables contract so that the fabric flares above and below, as shown in swatch **1**. To counteract this, make increases at the base of the cables and decreases at the top. In swatch **2**, five stitches were cast on for each six-stitch cable. On the wrong-side row before the first cable row, each of these sets of stitches was worked p3, m1p, p2, so that the increase was hidden behind the subsequent cable cross. On the wrong-side row following the last cables each of the cables was worked p1, p2tog, p3 to return to five stitches. This can be adapted to suit any cables, but position the shapings so that they do not show.

Gathering-in fullness

A large number of decreases will gather a piece of knitting, but it looks more elegant if the decreases can be integrated into the stitch pattern. Here, two four-row repeats of seaweed (see page 103) were followed by a right-side row consisting of k1, [skpo twice, p1, skpo twice, k2tog, p1, k2tog] to last st, k1. This reduced each fourteen-stitch repeat to eight stitches while retaining the line of the ribs.

Using a single-row repeat as an edging

Rows one to sixteen of bunches of cherries (see page 124) make a lovely scalloped edging to plain stockinette stitch. To prevent the stockinette stitch from spreading, double decreases have been worked along the seventeenth row, reducing each stitch repeat to eighteen stitches: [k9, s2kpo, k8] to last st, k1. Beginning with a purl row, continue in stockinette stitch.

Compensating for an undulating edge

If you're working a chevron stitch pattern and don't want a wavy cast-off edge, you'll need to fill in each dip separately by decreasing instead of increasing at each side while still working the decreases at the center. Depending on yarn and gauge, you may need to decrease on wrong-side rows as well.

Gallery of ideas

Here are some miniature knits (knitdowns) to spark ideas for projects. They are simplified illustrations of just a few of the techniques needed to create your own garments and accessories.

Flared shapes
To create such a shape, start with a wide rib at the lower edge and decrease to a simple 2 × 2 rib for the yoke. For a neat effect, work the decreases at the edges of the wide rib panels on wrong-side rows, pairing them k2tog and skpo so that they will hardly show on the right side.

Shaping in lace
Here, a simple lace pattern, baby shale (see page 84), shows how omitting the yarn overs on the last row reduces the number of stitches and in this design draws in the fabric under the bust. To shape in a lace pattern, it is important to distinguish between the increases and decreases that make the design and the increases or decreases that shape the item.

Measuring for a hat
Translate the measurement around your head into stitches. Underestimate rather than overestimate the stitches because the knitting will stretch. Adjust these stitches to a number that will divide into four segments for shaping the crown, with one stitch between each segment. Each segment is then decreased with skpo on one side and k2tog on the other. The last few stitches are gathered up at the top.

Design freedom
This scarf is slightly unconventional because it's simply a four-stitch cable without edgings. It starts on three stitches with an increase concealed below the first cable and a decrease tucked in after the last cable. If you adapt the idea for yourself using bulky yarn, make sure the yarn will press so you can eliminate the tendency of the cable to curl.

Knitting in the round
The classic way to knit a sock is in the round to avoid an uncomfortable seam. Once you understand the principle, it's not difficult to work from the top, hold the instep stitches while you turn the heel, then pick up from the side of the heel and proceed to the toe shaping. There are many methods of shaping the heel and toe, so following a set of simple instructions is probably the best way to begin.

Shaping with increases and decreases
A purse can be so expressive. This one has increases along the first row, followed by a few increases at the sides to create a pouchy shape. After working a large bobble center front, the top is drawn in with a few decreases and the flap made. A pick-up and bind-off row along the edges reinforces the sides and continues as a handle. A stitched loop catches the bobble to make a fastening that could easily be adapted for clothing.

Combining color patterns
Choose stitches that add up to the largest multiple, such as the combination of four-and-eight stitch repeats used here. To work in the round from the color charts, simply omit the edge stitches and read the repeat stitches from right to left for every round. To shape a circular yoke, you can either decrease between bands of pattern or decrease between motifs.

Essential techniques

If you're a new knitter, you will find here all the information you need to get started and maybe even enough to attempt more ambitious stitches.

SLIPKNOT

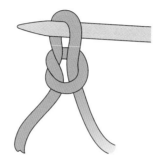

1 Putting a slipknot on the needle makes the first stitch of the cast-on. Loop the yarn around two fingers of the left hand, the ball end on top. Dip the needle into the loop, catch the ball end of the yarn, and pull it through the loop.

2 Pull the ends of the yarn to tighten the knot. Tighten the ball end to bring the knot up to the needle.

Ends

The end of yarn left after casting on should be a reasonable length so that it can be used for sewing up. The same applies to the end left after binding off. Ends left when a new color is joined in should be darned in along a seam or row end on the wrong side and can also be very useful for covering up imperfections, such as awkward color changes. Ends left while working a motif are better darned in behind the motif. Use a blunt-pointed tapestry needle for darning in.

LONG-TAIL CAST-ON

This uses a single needle and produces an elastic knitted edge like a row of garter stitch.

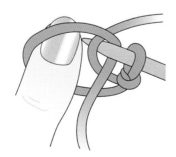

1 Leaving an end about three times the length of the required cast-on, put a slipknot on the needle. Holding the yarn end in the left hand, take the left thumb under the yarn and upward. Insert the needle in the loop just made on the thumb.

2 Use the ball end of the yarn to make a knit stitch, slipping the loop off the thumb. Pull the yarn end to close the stitch up to the needle. Continue making stitches in this way.

CHAIN BIND-OFF

A simple knit-stitch bind-off is used in most of these projects. Knit two stitches. * With the left needle, lift the first stitch over the second. Knit the next stitch. Repeat from * until one stitch remains. Break the yarn, take the end through this stitch, and tighten.

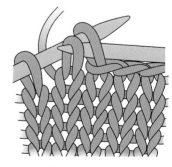

To bind off in pattern, simply work knit or purl stitches along the bind-off row as they would occur in the stitch pattern.

KNIT STITCH (K)

Choose to hold the yarn and needles in whichever way you feel most comfortable. To tension the yarn—that is, to keep it moving evenly—you will need to twist it through some fingers of the hand holding the yarn, and maybe even take it around your little finger. Continuous rows of knit stitch produce garter stitch.

1 Insert the right needle into the first stitch on the left needle. Make sure it goes from left to right into the front of the stitch.

2 Taking the yarn behind, bring it up and around the right needle.

3 Using the tip of the right needle, draw a loop of yarn through the stitch.

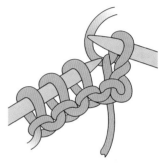

4 Slip the stitch off the left needle. There is now a new stitch on the right needle.

PURL STITCH (P)

Hold the yarn and needles in the same way as for making a knit stitch. A purl stitch is the exact opposite of a knit stitch, producing a nubbly stitch to the front and a smooth V-like knit stitch on the opposite side. Alternate rows of knit and purl produce stockinette stitch.

1 Insert the right needle into the first stitch on the left needle. Make sure it goes into the stitch from right to left.

2 Taking the yarn to the front, loop it around the right needle.

3 Lower the tip of the right needle, taking it away from you to draw a loop of yarn through the stitch.

4 Slip the stitch off the left needle. There is now a new stitch on the right needle.

Essential techniques—continued

DECREASES
Decreases have two basic functions. They can be used to reduce the number of stitches in a row, as in armholes and necklines, and combined with increases, they can create stitch patterns.

Right-slanting single decrease (k2tog)
Knitting two stitches together makes a smooth shaping, with the second stitch lying on top of the first.

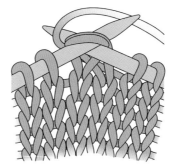

1 Insert the right needle through the front of the first two stitches on the left needle, then take the yarn around the needle.

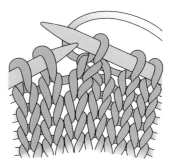

2 Draw the loop through and drop the two stitches off the left needle.

Left-slanting single decrease (skpo)
Slipping a stitch, knitting a stitch, then lifting the slipped stitch over the knit stitch makes a decrease, with the first stitch lying on top of the second.

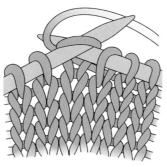

1 Insert the right needle knitwise through the front of the first stitch on the left needle, and slip it on to the right. Knit the next stitch.

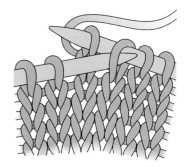

2 Use the tip of the left needle to lift the slipped stitch over the knitted stitch and off the right needle.

Left-slanting double decrease (sk2po)
For a double decrease that slants to the left, worked on a right-side row, you'll need to take the first stitch over a single decrease.

For a similar-looking decrease worked on a wrong-side row, purl three together through the back of the loops (p3tog tbl).

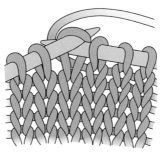

1 Insert the right needle knitwise through the front of the first stitch on the left needle, and slip it on to the right needle.

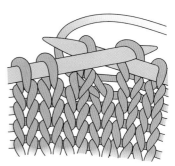

2 Knit the next two stitches together, then lift the first stitch over as shown. To make a right-slanting double decrease, simply knit three stitches together (k3tog).

Balanced double decrease (s2kpo)

Working a decrease that takes one stitch from each side and leaves the center stitch on top has lots of potential for shaping and for working beautiful stitch patterns.

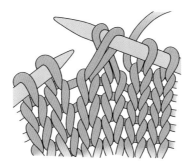

1 Insert the right needle into the second and first stitches as if to knit two together, and slip these stitches on to the right needle.

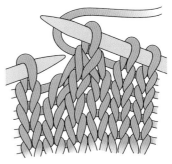

2 Knit the next stitch, then lift the two slipped stitches over.

CABLES

Knitting groups of stitches out of sequence creates exciting stitch patterns. Cables can be worked with two or more stitches and crossed to the front or the back.

Front cable (c4f)

The stitches in this example are knitted, and this four-stitch cable crosses at the front. A four-stitch back cable (c4b) is worked in exactly the same way, except that the cable needle is held at the back, so that the cable crosses in the opposite direction.

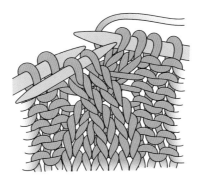

1 Slip the first two stitches on to a cable needle and hold at the front of the work, then knit the next two stitches from the left needle.

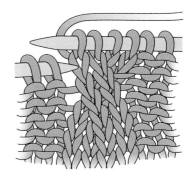

2 Knit the two stitches from the cable needle.

YARN OVER (YO)

It's essential to take the yarn over the needle so that the strand lies in the same direction as the other stitches. Working into this strand on the next row makes a hole, but if the strand is twisted, the hole will close up.

When the stitch before a yarn over is purl, the yarn will already be at the front, ready to go over the needle.

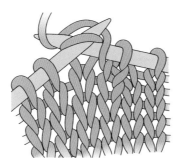

1 To make a yarn over between knit stitches, bring the yarn to the front as if to purl, then take it over the needle to knit the next stitch.

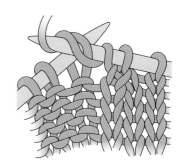

2 To make a yarn over between a knit and a purl, bring the yarn to the front as if to purl, take it over the needle, and bring it to the front again, ready to purl.

Essential techniques—continued

INCREASES
Here are two of the most basic methods of increasing a single stitch—bar increase and lifted strand increase.

Bar increase on a knit row (kfb)
Knitting into the front and the back of a stitch is the most common increase. It's a neat, firm increase, which makes a little bar on the right side of the work at the base of the new stitch. This makes it easy to count rows between shapings and doesn't leave a hole.

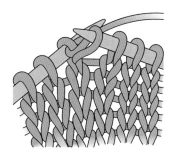

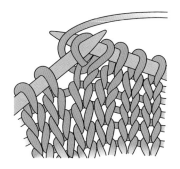

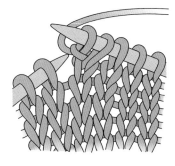

1 Knit into the front of the stitch and pull the loop through, but leave the stitch on the left needle.

2 Knit into the back of the stitch on the left needle.

3 Slip the stitch off the left needle, making two stitches on the right needle. Note that the bar of the new stitch lies on the left.

Lifted strand increase to the left (m1 or m1L)
Making a stitch from the strand between stitches is a very neat way to increase.

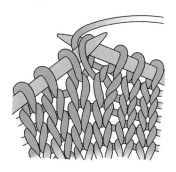

From the front, insert the left needle under the strand between stitches. Make sure the strand lies on the needle in the same direction as the other stitches, then knit into the back of it.

Lifted strand increase to the right (m1R)
This right-slanting increase balances exactly the lifted strand increase to the left.

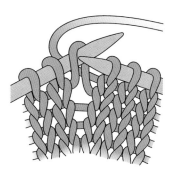

From the back, insert the left needle under the strand between the stitches. It will not lie in the same direction as the other stitches, so knit into the front of it.

Double increase
This is one of the simplest ways to make three stitches out of one.

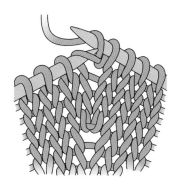

Knit one stitch without slipping it off, take the yarn over the right needle from front to back, then knit the same stitch again. A small but decorative hole is left in the fabric.

TWISTS

Twisting stitches is working two or three stitches out of sequence, but without using a cable needle. This is an easy way to create patterns where lines of stitches travel over the surface of the knitting.

Left twist (t2L)

This twist is worked on a right-side row. As the stitches change place, the first stitch lies on top and slants to the left, while the stitch behind is worked through the back of the loop.

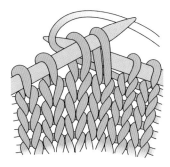
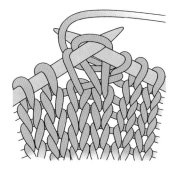
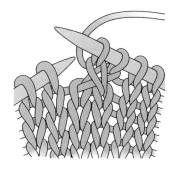

1 Knit into the back of the second stitch.

2 Knit into the front of the first stitch.

3 Slip both stitches off the left needle together.

Right twist (t2R)

In this right-sided row twist, the second stitch lies on top and slants to the right, while the stitch behind is worked through the back of the loop.

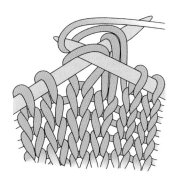
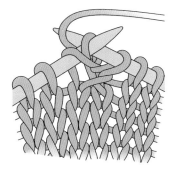
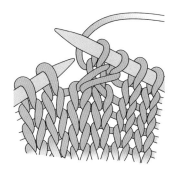

1 Knit into the front of the second stitch.

2 Knit into the back of the first stitch.

3 Slip both stitches off the left needle together.

Reading the charts

Showing stitch patterns as charts is a visual explanation of how to work them; the symbols are used to create a stylized picture. Most of the stitch-pattern sections contain a few examples that have both charts and written-out instructions. These will help you relate the symbols to the words that describe the stitches. You will find that one of the advantages of charted stitch patterns is that it is possible to show large designs that would be repetitive and difficult to follow if written out in full.

DUAL-PURPOSE SYMBOLS

Because the stitch patterns in this book are designed to be worked in rows, some of the symbols have two functions. For instance, a blank square should be read as knit on a right-side row and purl on a wrong-side row; a square with a dot should be read as purl on a right-side row and knit on a wrong-side row.

READING ORDER

Each chart should be read from the lower edge upward, progressing in the same way as the work, with each row of squares on the chart representing a row of knitting. All right-side rows are read from right to left, and all wrong-side rows are read from left to right. The rows are numbered, and in most cases the first and odd-numbered rows are right-side rows (starting with the number 1 on the right). Occasionally charts start with a wrong-side row, so the number 1 and all odd numbers are on the left. After all the rows of the chart have been worked, start again at the first row to continue the pattern, or at the row specified, if there are set-up rows.

Simple stitch chart
The chart of this simple stitch shows clearly that while knit and purl stitches on right-side rows form the pattern, all wrong-side rows are purled.

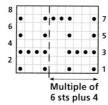

Multiple of
6 sts plus 4

Reading from right to left and left to right
If right-side rows are not read from right to left and wrong-side rows from left to right, this sample stitch pattern won't form diagonals.

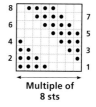

Multiple of
8 sts

BEFORE YOU START

Read through your chosen chart before starting to knit to make sure that you understand how to work the symbols used to create the stitch pattern. Check also for any other requirements. For instance, for all stitch patterns in the cable section, you'll need a cable needle, but if a cable needle is required in other sections, the instructions will state this. The most frequently used symbols are shown as "Basic symbols" at the foot of the page. Symbols that occur occasionally or are worked in a particular way for a particular chart are given as "Specific symbols" with the chart itself.

VARIABLE STITCH COUNTS

Some stitch patterns do not have the same number of stitches on every row. If there are shaded squares or areas on the chart, do not count any stitches for these areas, they are there to compensate for stitches made or lost within the design. A shaded square in the list of symbols is simply called "no stitch."

SUPPLEMENTARY CHARTS

A chart may have separate supplementary charts, for instance, to show leaves (see page 117). The row numbers on the supplementary chart correspond to the numbers outlined on the main chart, and each row should be worked in the position indicated. When casting on for stitch patterns with a variable stitch count, always cast on the multiple given, ignoring any shaded areas and if stated, adding any extra stitches given for the supplementary chart, plus edge stitches.

Working with separate charts
The stitches outlined over seven rows in the center of the main chart are numbered to correspond with the rows of the seven-row supplementary chart.

Check out the charts
The specific symbol is worked over two stitches and a yarn over and applies to this chart only.

Multiple of
4 sts plus 2

No-stitch symbols
All the rows of this blackberry-stitch pattern (see page 25) have four stitches, but the double increases and double decreases on the second and fourth rows require shaded areas to compensate.

Multiple of 4 sts

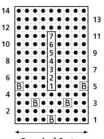

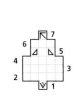

Panel of 9 sts,
with a variable
st count

Reading the charts—continued

FOLLOWING REPEATS

For panels or motifs, the number of stitches is written underneath the chart. For allover design, the pattern is given as a multiple of stitches plus one or more stitches. To cast on for a swatch, multiply the number of stitches for the repeat two or more times and then add on the edge stitch or stitches. On the chart, the number of stitches to repeat is indicated by an arrow underneath the chart and vertical broken lines in the chart. Where there is just one broken line, on a right-side row, work the repeat stitches as many times as needed, then work the stitch(es) beyond the broken line once to complete the row. On a wrong-side row, work the stitch(es) before the broken line once, then work the repeat stitch(es) as many times as needed to complete the row.

Broken lines on right- and wrong-side rows

When there are two broken lines, on both right- and wrong-side rows, work the stitch(es) shown before the broken line once, work the repeat stitches the number of times needed, and then work the stitch(es) beyond the broken line once to complete the row.

Broken lines going through a group of stitches

If the broken lines showing the repeat go through a group of stitches worked together, such as a cable, continue working the rest of the action as marked off at each side of the broken lines, and then complete the row with the remaining edge stitches.

Connecting lines

To make the charts easier to follow, additional lines may connect one symbol with another, say, between cables, but this doesn't affect how the stitches are worked.

One edge stitch
This chart shows just one edge stitch on the left.

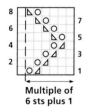

Multiple of
6 sts plus 1

Neat finish
The edge stitches here make a neat finish at each side of this four-stitch repeat pattern.

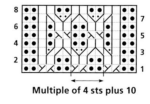

Multiple of 4 sts plus 10

Connecting lines and cables
Additional vertical lines connect the four-stitch cables to make this chart easier to follow.

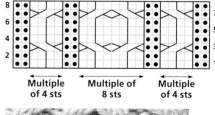

| Multiple of 4 sts | Multiple of 8 sts | Multiple of 4 sts |

COLOR KNITTING

Color charts are read in the same way as stockinette-stitch charts with every right-side row knit and every wrong-side row purl, using colors as shown. There are two methods of color knitting, stranded knitting and intarsia. In stranded color knitting, the yarns used are continuous and the yarn not in use is carried across on the wrong side of the work. It is used for small or regular repeats.

Stranded knitting
When working these tiny patterns, you never need to carry the yarn over more than three stitches.

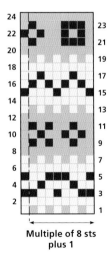

Multiple of 8 sts
plus 1

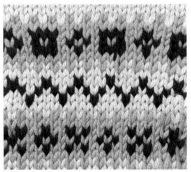

Choosing the method

Intarsia is used for larger areas of color, with a small ball or length of yarn used for each different color area. When changing colors, cross the yarns firmly to link them. If you must strand across a large area of color, weave the second yarn in on the wrong side, but be aware that this will thicken the fabric. Some designs are best worked in a mixture of stranded and intarsia techniques.

Intarsia
Although there is a small amount of stranded knitting around the knot of the bow, most of this design has been worked in intarsia, since the areas of color are too large to carry yarn across.

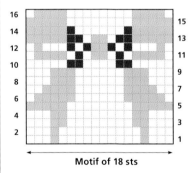

Motif of 18 sts

Abbreviations and symbols

Frequently used abbreviated knitting terms and symbols are provided below and opposite. Any unusual abbreviations or symbols—specific to a particular stitch pattern—are presented as "Specific symbols" alongside the relevant chart.

Abbreviations

c2b	sl1 st on to cable needle, hold at back, k1, then k1 from cable needle
c2bp	sl1 st on to cable needle, hold at back, k1, then p1 from cable needle
c2f	sl1 st on to cable needle, hold at front, k1, then k1 from cable needle
c2fp	sl1 st on to cable needle, hold at front, p1, then k1 from cable needle
c3b	sl1 st on to cable needle, hold at back, k2, then k1 from cable needle
c3bp	sl1 st on to cable needle, hold at back, k2, then p1 from cable needle
c3f	sl2 sts on to cable needle, hold at front, k1, then k2 from cable needle
c3fp	sl2 sts on to cable needle, hold at front, p1, then k2 from cable needle
c4b	sl2 sts on to cable needle, hold at back, k2, then k2 from cable needle
c4bp	sl2 sts on to cable needle, hold at back, k2, then p2 from cable needle
c4f	sl2 sts on to cable needle, hold at front, k2, then k2 from cable needle
c4fp	sl2 sts on to cable needle, hold at front, p2, then k2 from cable needle
c5bp	sl2 sts on to cable needle, hold at back, k3, then p2 from cable needle
c5fp	sl3 sts on to cable needle, hold at front, p2, then k3 from cable needle
c6b	sl3 sts on to cable needle, hold at back, k3, then k3 from cable needle
c6bp	sl3 sts on to cable needle, hold at back, k3, then p3 from cable needle
c6f	slip 3 sts on to cable needle, hold at front, k3, then k3 from cable needle
c6fp	sl3 sts on to cable needle, hold at front, p3, then k3 from cable needle

cont	continue
k	knit
k1b	k next st in row below
kfb	k into front and back of st
k2tog	knit 2 together
L	left
mb	make bobble as directed
m1	as m1L
m1L	using left needle, lift strand between sts from front and k this tbl to make st that slants to left
m1p	using left needle, lift strand between sts from front and p this tbl
m1R	using left needle, lift strand between sts from back and k in front of it to make st that slants to right
p	purl
p1b	purl next st in row below
pfb	purl into front and back of st
psso	pass slipped st over
R	right
rem	remaining
rep	repeat
RS	right side
s2kpo	sl2 sts as if to k2tog, k1, pass slipped sts over
skpo	sl1 st knitwise, k1, pass slipped st over
sk2po	sl1 st knitwise, k2tog, pass slipped st over
sl	slip
ssp	sl 1st st knitwise, then 2nd st knitwise, return sts to left needle, noting that they now face in the opposite direction, swing right needle round to insert it in 2nd st, then 1st st and p2tog
st(s)	stitch(es)

St st	stockinette st		**WS**	wrong side
tbl	through back of loop(s)		**wyab**	with yarn at back
tfl	through front of loop(s)		**wyif**	with yarn in front
tog	together		**yb**	take yarn between needles to back of work
t2L	k into back of 2nd st, then k into front of 1st st, sl both sts off left needle tog		**yf**	take yarn between needles to front of work
t2Lp	on RS and on WS, p into back of 2nd st, then k into front of 1st st, sl both sts off left needle tog		**yo**	yarn over needle (see *Essential techniques*, page 197)
t2R	k into front of 2nd st, then k into back of 1st st, sl both sts off left needle tog		**[ ]**	repeat instructions in square brackets as directed
t2Rp	on RS, k into front of 2nd st, then p into front of 1st st, sl both sts off left needle tog; on WS, k into front of 2nd st, then p into back of 1st st, sl both sts off left needle tog		**( )**	parentheses indicate a group of sts worked in 1 st

Symbols

□	k on RS, p on WS			t2Rp or c2bp
●	p on RS, k on WS			t2L or c2f
	k tbl on RS, p tbl on WS			t2Lp or c2fp
	k2tog			c3b
	skpo			c3bp
	p2tog			c3f
	s2kpo			c3fp
	k3tog			c4b
	sk2po			c4bp
	m1			c4f
	m1p			c4fp
	m1L			c5bp
	m1R			c5fp
O	yarn over needle (see *Essential techniques*, page 197)			c6b
	no stitch (see *Reading the charts*, page 201)			c6bp
	kfb			c6f
	pfb			c6fp
	t2R or c2b			

Index

Abbreviations

c2b	sl1 st on to cable needle, hold at back, k1, then k1 from cable needle
c2bp	sl1 st on to cable needle, hold at back, k1, then p1 from cable needle
c2f	sl1 st on to cable needle, hold at front, k1, then k1 from cable needle
c2fp	sl1 st on to cable needle, hold at front, p1, then k1 from cable needle
c3b	sl1 st on to cable needle, hold at back, k2, then k1 from cable needle
c3bp	sl1 st on to cable needle, hold at back, k2, then p1 from cable needle
c3f	sl2 sts on to cable needle, hold at front, k1, then k2 from cable needle
c3fp	sl2 sts on to cable needle, hold at front, p1, then k2 from cable needle
c4b	sl2 sts on to cable needle, hold at back, k2, then k2 from cable needle
c4bp	sl2 sts on to cable needle, hold at back, k2, then p2 from cable needle
c4f	sl2 sts on to cable needle, hold at front, k2, then k2 from cable needle
c4fp	sl2 sts on to cable needle, hold at front, p2, then k2 from cable needle
c5bp	sl2 sts on to cable needle, hold at back, k3, then p2 from cable needle
c5fp	sl3 sts on to cable needle, hold at front, p2, then k3 from cable needle
c6b	sl3 sts on to cable needle, hold at back, k3, then k3 from cable needle
c6bp	sl3 sts on to cable needle, hold at back, k3, then p3 from cable needle
c6f	sl3 sts on to cable needle, hold at front, k3, then k3 from cable needle
c6fp	sl3 sts on to cable needle, hold at front, p3, then k3 from cable needle
cont	continue
k	knit
k1b	k next st in row below
kfb	k into front and back of st
k2tog	knit 2 together
L	left
mb	make bobble as directed
m1	as m1L
m1L	using L needle, lift strand between sts from front and k this tbl to make st that slants to left
m1p	using L needle, lift strand between sts from front and p this tbl
m1R	using L needle, lift strand between sts from back and k in front of it to make st that slants to right
p	purl
p1b	purl next st in row below
pfb	purl into front and back of st
psso	pass slipped st over
R	right
rem	remaining
rep	repeat
RS	right side
s2kpo	sl next 2 sts as if to k2tog, k1, pass slipped sts over
skpo	sl1 st knitwise, k1, pass slipped st over
sk2po	sl1 st knitwise, k2tog, pass slipped st over
sl	slip
ssp	sl 1st st knitwise, then 2nd st knitwise, return sts to L needle, noting that they now face in the opposite direction, swing R needle round to insert it in 2nd st, then 1st st and p2tog
st(s)	stitch(es)
St st	stockinette st
tbl	through back of loop(s)
tfl	through front of loop(s)
tog	together
t2L	k into back of 2nd st, then k into front of 1st st, sl both sts off L needle tog
t2Lp	on RS and on WS, p into back of 2nd st, then k into front of 1st st, sl both sts off L needle tog
t2R	k into front of 2nd st, then k into back of 1st st, sl both sts off L needle tog
t2Rp	on RS, k into front of 2nd st, then p into front of 1st st, sl both sts off L needle tog, on WS, k into front of 2nd st, then p into back of 1st st, sl both sts off L needle tog
WS	wrong side
wyab	with yarn at back
wyif	with yarn in front
yb	take yarn between needles to back of work
yf	take yarn between needles to front of work
yo	yarn over needle (see *Essential techniques*, page 194)
[ ]	repeat instructions in square brackets as directed
( )	parentheses indicate a group of sts worked in 1 st

Fold-out flap

Fold out this flap while you knit, for an at-a-glance reminder of the abbreviations used in the pattern instructions. Below is a useful needle-size conversion chart.

International needle sizes

Metric (mm) Europe	US	UK/ Canada/Australia	Japan/ China
2.0	0	14	—
2.10	—	—	—
2.25	1	13	—
2.40	—	—	1
2.70	—	—	2
2.75	2	12	—
3.0	—	11	3
3.25	3	10	—
3.30	—	—	4
3.5	4	—	—
3.60	—	—	5
3.75	5	9	—
3.90	—	—	—
4.0	6	8	—
4.20	—	—	7
4.5	7	7	8
4.80	—	—	9
5.0	8	6	—
5.10	—	—	10
5.40	—	—	11
5.5	9	5	—
5.70	—	—	12
6.0	10	4	13
6.30	—	—	14
6.5	10½	3	—
6.60	—	—	15
7.0	—	2	—
7.5	—	1	—
8.0	11	0	—
9.0	13	00	—
10.0	15	000	—
12.75	17	—	—
15.0	19	—	—
19.0	35	—	—
25.0	50	—	—

Credits

With special thanks to Susan Horan for her contribution to this book, and Brown Sheep Company, Inc., Debbie Bliss, and Sublime Yarns for supplying the beautiful yarns used in this book.

Brown Sheep Company, Inc.
100662 County Road 16
Mitchell, Nebraska 69357
tel: 1 800 826 9136
fax: 1 308 635 2143
www.brownsheep.com

Debbie Bliss
Designer Yarns Limited
Unit 8–10
Newbridge Industrial Estate
Pitt Street, Keighley
West Yorkshire, BD21 4PQ
tel: +44 (0)1535 664 222
fax: +44 (0)1535 664 333
www.designeryarns.uk.com

Sublime Yarns
Flanshaw Lane
Wakefield
West Yorkshire, WF2 9ND
tel: +44 (0) 1924 231 686
contactus@sublimeyarns.com

In Memoriam: Melody Griffiths

The Essential Stitch Collection is dedicated to the memory of author Melody Griffiths, who passed away in the final stages of the book's production. Melody was an exceptional designer and author, a true professional, and above all a wonderful friend. She is greatly missed.